# inevitable Too!

## The Total Leader Embraces Mass Customized Learning

Charles Schwahn & Beatrice McGarvey

# Introduction

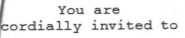

You are
cordially invited to

**TRANSFORM EDUCATION**

Acceptances Only:
www.masscustomizedlearning.com

# OUR JOURNEY: Chuck's Perspective

As Bea and I begin to write *Inevitable Too!  The Total Leader Embraces Mass Customized Learning*, allow me a bit of boastful history. The first part of my story begins in 1998 when the American Association of School Administrators (AASA) asked my great friend and colleague, Dr. William Spady, and me to write a "leadership book." We had been touring the US and Canada for some time talking with educators about leadership, the change process, outcome-based education, future focusing, and strategic design. The topics were popular, we were considered somewhat expert.  Our book *Total Leaders: Applying the Best Future-Focused Change Strategies to Education* was a hit.  So much of a hit that in 2010 AASA asked Bill and me to write a new edition of our leadership book, and we did.  And so, *Total Leaders 2.0: Leading in the Age of Empowerment* came to be, and is doing quite well also.

The second part of my story involves my friend and colleague Bea McGarvey. We both had been working with schools and districts around the country on various topics in "school reform." Fast forward a few decades and we were concerned and cranky. We realized that, along with most school reformers, we had been *tinkering* with mere blips of improvement. We also knew the wall that all educators inevitably (ahem) faced with all of these reforms was the time-based structure inherited from the Industrial Age.

Energized by our concern and crankiness, we decided to *save the world of education* by proposing a vision for learners and learning that rids school systems of the Industrial Age assembly-line structure, and replaces it with an Information Age structure that we chose to label "mass customized learning." We titled our book, our vision, *Inevitable: Mass Customized Learning*.  And as somewhat of a surprise, *Inevitable* has created a buzz throughout the education community.  Nearly everyone who reads it knows that it is the right thing to do, they find the vision very desirable, and most see the vision as "doable."

The third and final part of my story also seems inevitable.  For the past year, our colleagues have hounded Bea and me to write a book that ties together *Total Leaders 2.0* and *Inevitable: Mass Customized Learning*. The purpose of this book is to do just that: to inspire and assist the Total Leader with the implementation of the mass customized learning vision. MCL provides the Total Leader with the vision – the place to go. And, *Total Leaders 2.0* describes the performance roles to get there.

If you were the perfect Total Leader, but didn't have a clear and compelling purpose and vision in mind, you would be missing half of what it takes to make a contribution to the world, and in this case, to the world of education.  And if you had a clear and compelling vision and purpose, but didn't have the leadership wisdom and skills to pull it off, you, too, would be missing a critical component of what it takes to make meaningful change happen.

Never fear, we are here to give you both the leadership and the vision to create the *Inevitable* educational system of the future, the Mass Customized Learning system that meets the learning needs of every learner every hour of every day. We are right now in the phone booth changing into our Superman and Superwoman outfits. Trust us, the world will be a better place.

## HOPE FOR THE FLOWERS: Bea's Perspective

While we were courting, over 35 years ago, my husband, Richard, gave me the book, *Hope for the Flowers* by Trina Paulus. It is a sweet, inspirational parable of hope, perseverance, and vision. As Chuck, I have been driven by a moral imperative to ensure that every learner enjoys success in school. That little book has always resonated with me. I love the title. I thought, "If I ever write a book about education, the title would be *There IS Hope for the Flowers.*" On a bad day of experiencing educational inertia, resisting staff, and if-it-ain't-broke thinking, however, I might have changed the title to *Is There Hope for the Flowers?*

Chuck and I have spent our entire careers as teachers, school and district administrators, and consultants trying to find a way to personalize learning for each learner. Our heroines and heroes are those teachers who personalize, customize learning in spite of the assembly-line structure of our schools. Sooner or later, however, teachers and principals run up against our "one-size-fits-all" instructional delivery structure and system. For Chuck, it began in the 60s, for me the 70s. We were disciples of Madeline Hunter, John Goodlad, Dwight Allen, Ted Sizer, Roland Barth, and Larry Lezotte. I do this name-dropping so you know how long we have hoped for and worked for real educational reform.

That 60s and 70s hope has grown exponentially. Our book, *Inevitable: Mass Customized Learning* has been very well received. More books are already in circulation than we could have dreamed. Nearly everyone finds the vision most desirable and doable. We think we know the reason for the vision's success MCL, as described in *Inevitable*, is the only vision that we are aware of that rids education of the stymieing Industrial Age assembly line. All other would-be innovators and reformers give in to the Industrial Age structure and end up proposing "tinkering changes" rather than to suggest real reform.

Well, yes, cyber schools that propose everything be learned online do rid themselves of the assembly line, but they too have a one-size-fits-all approach for learners. Instinctively, we educators know that is not the way to go. The MCL Vision keeps what we know works in education and replaces those structures and practices that block real educational transformation. MCL does not "throw out the baby with the bathwater."

The wide acceptance of the MCL Vision brings new hope. More tangibly, learning that the Lindsay Unified School District in California has received one of ten Race to the Top grants from the US Office of Education for a proposal based on the Mass Customized Learning Vision lifts our hopes even higher. Lindsay has a good shot at making MCL a reality . . . strong, committed, and passionate leadership, a changing culture supportive of learners and learning, and $10 million to make it happen.

Lindsay is using all of the components in this book. They are applying the Total Leaders Framework as their leadership model, they used our Strategic Design process for setting their direction and the MCL Vision as their picture of what they will look like, feel like, and be like when operating at their ideal best. Visit Lindsay's website **www.lindsay.k12.ca.us** to see their Strategic Direction – their covenant.

And so, I say with great confidence and conviction *there IS hope for the flowers.*

## ABOUT THE BOOK

We have organized the book as follows:

**Introduction:**  Gives the whys, the whats, and the hows of our thinking to align your thinking with the structure of *Inevitable Too! The Total Leader Embraces Mass Customized Learning.*

**Chapter 1:**  **Total Leaders**
Gives a short version of the Total Leaders Framework.

**Chapter 2:**  **The Mass Customized Learning Vision**
Gives a short version of the Mass Customized Learning Vision. If you have not read either or both of these books, you might find time to read and, hopefully, study them. Both *Total Leaders 2.0* and *Inevitable* have been frequently used as the basis for book studies by leadership teams and by school staffs.

Each of the following five chapters will focus on one of the Leadership Domains and Pillars of Change that are at the heart of the Total Leaders Framework.

**Chapter 3:**  **The Authentic Leader Creates a Reason to Change**
Applies the 3 Performance Roles of the Authentic Leader to create a REASON for the Mass Customized Learning Vision

# ABOUT OUR WRITING

We close our introduction with a note or two about how we do things as a team. First, we take our work very seriously. We believe very strongly that education must change. We believe today's learning opportunities and teaching challenges are unfair to learners and teachers alike. But, we don't take ourselves very seriously. We insist on having some fun while writing. Heavy topics, presented lightly. Neither of us thinks of our self as a writer or as an author. We think of ourselves as visionaries who communicate effectively . . . we think! Writing does not come easy, but our guilt pushes us forward.

We have learned that words we use control the way we think. We want our readers to think of our "students" as "learners." We *get* students to learn, but we *facilitate* learning because it's natural. We want our readers to think "learning facilitators" rather than teachers; to think "seminars" with flexible starting and ending times rather than courses; "learning opportunities" rather than classes or lectures, etc. We are seeing new and expansive vocabularies changing the culture of ~~schools~~ learning communities.

We will try to consistently use what we believe to be a mind and behavior changing vocabulary as we communicate with you.

We are a team, and we write as one. We will use "we" when referring to things we have "teamed on" and will use "I" and our initials (cjs or bmcg) when we relate personal stories. And to stay away from the clumsy "he/she," we will use either "he" or "she" randomly. Those of you who are more politically correct than we may want to count the "hes" and "shes" as you read along.

# ACKNOWLEDGEMENTS

## From Chuck:

*Bill Spady has been my teammate for years. He is my friend, my colleague, my learning coach, and my mentor. Bill, (who may be "Dr. William Spady" to many of you) is my Total Leaders 2.0 co-author, and his lifetime Outcome-Based Education contributions are, in large part, the bedrock of Inevitable: Mass Customized Learning. Inevitable Too! is based on those two works, and my friend's influence clearly shows itself throughout. Thanks, Bill.*

*When Inevitable: MCL was still in an 8 ½ x 11 format, I walked into the TIE (Technology and Innovation in Education) office and met my new best friend, Jim Parry. Neither of our lives has been the same since. TIE has been a major force in the success of Inevitable. Jim, Julie Mathiesen, John Swanson, and Joe Hauge make up what I have labeled the TIE "J Squad." Their expertise, commitment, and professionalism have made the MCL Vision known, understood, and valued. We have been very good for each other . . . and for education.*

*These acknowledgements help me to realize how much we owe our supportive colleagues. Years ago I worked with and for PLDC (Pennsylvania Leadership Development Center) and met three men, then superintendents, who became friends, colleagues, and super supports. We "clicked" from the start and continue "clicking" in most everything we do. Pat Crawford, Duff Rearick, and Jay Scott have spread the Total Leaders Framework and the MCL Vision throughout PA and their region. Pat, Duff, and Jay have had a significant influence on Inevitable Too! Our influence goes in both directions.*

*Can't say enough about Genny, my bride for 50+. My love, my support, my encourager, and my editor. Genny and Bea ~~suggested~~ forced me to do Inevitable Too!; my colleague Bea McGarvey was already committed. Bea is a great friend and teammate. We bring different things to the table, we sync, and we synergize. Our passion for meeting learner needs and transforming education is shared.*

# From Bea:

*I begin my acknowledgements with a "ditto" to Chuck's remarks. The MCL Vision is a grassroots movement powered by the commitment and expertise of leaders like those at TIE and PLDC. They are making and will make MCL a reality!*

*How blessed I was to begin my journey — a few decades ago - around customizing learning at the Reiche School in Portland, Maine teaming with incredibly gifted teachers to implement Project P.L.A.N. (Programmed Learning According to Needs), an individualized learning, computer supported program developed by Westinghouse Corporation. We were pioneers. Teachers, Mary MacVane, Barbara Tracy, Margaret Douglass, Jeaneen Coleman, Nancy Sullivan, and others, taught me <u>how to teach</u>. Richard McGarvey, Reiche's first principal, influenced, and continues to influence, the values and principles which are the bedrock of our MCL Vision. He was a "total leader" when TL was a mere twinkle in Chuck's eye. As my principal, Mr. McGarvey taught me <u>about courageous, visionary leadership</u>. As my husband, he is my rock, my supporter, and my partner in all things.*

*The work of Robert Marzano and Debra Pickering runs through my veins! Their research, writings, and presentations have influenced my thinking and practice. Decades ago, with enormous respect and awe, I became a student of their work. Today, I am proud and grateful to be their colleague and friend. The MCL Vision grew out of the research on learning and is built on the assumption of effective instruction. Bob and Debra have taught me — and continue to teach me - <u>about the nature of learning, the nature of knowledge, and effective teaching</u>.*

*And finally, I am grateful for that day decades ago, when Ken Murphy, then Superintendent in Yarmouth, Maine, insisted that I attend a presentation being made to his entire staff by Dr. Charles Schwahn. It was a defining moment for me. Chuck has influenced, mentored, and supported me beyond words. Often, I say a little "Thanks for that day" prayer.*

# Chapter 1

# Total Leaders

*Applying the Best Future-Focused Change Strategies to Education*

# INTERACTIVE TL 2.0 FRAMEWORK

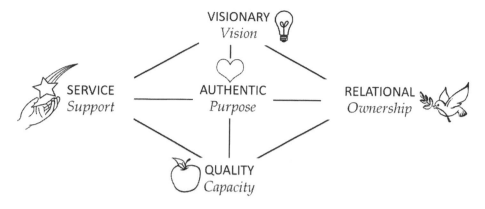

**Figure 1.2**

## STRATEGIC DESIGN

> *"If you want to make God laugh out loud . . .*
> *tell him about YOUR plan!"*
>
> **Author Unknown**

(cjs) *When Dr. William Spady and I created our Strategic Design process, we decided not to call it "Strategic Planning," as that term was being used to identify real strategic plans, but it was also being used to refer to notes on the back of a bar napkin. We wanted to define our terms, so we looked for new terms whose definitions had not been bastardized. We wanted to be clear, that school district plans were not "strategic" unless they were:*

> ▶ *Learner-centered,*

> ▶ *Based upon our best research regarding learners and learning,*

> ▶ *Future-focused.*

*For us, and for our clients, "being strategic" means we would not focus first on the needs of educators. It would ask, "How is this learner outcome best learned?" rather than "How is this outcome best taught?" And, the planning would be based upon the challenges and opportunities learners are expected to face after they leave our school. In short, strategic planning would begin and end with a clear focus on learners and learning.*

Figure 1.3 introduces clients to the TL 2.0 Framework. We title this simple diagram Leadership 101, as in the first day of your first course on leadership. Note that this figure is actually the top three boxes of the Figure 1.1, Linear TL 2.0 Framework. The bulleted listing under Strategic Direction identifies where the organization is heading, and the listing under Strategic Alignment identifies the four most critical aspects of the organization that must be made to "align" with that direction if the organization is to accomplish its Strategic Direction.

## LEADERSHIP 101

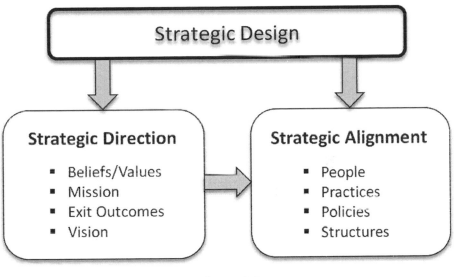

**Figure 1.3**

Figure 1.4 defines the four components of a comprehensive Strategic Direction. These four statements/documents will serve as the decision screen for all-important decisions. They are your governance. They give power and legitimacy to the work.

---

Components of a
**STRATEGIC DIRECTION**

**Values/Beliefs/Guiding Principles**
*What we honor & believe . . . therefore, how we do things*

**Mission**
*Why we exist; what business we are in*

**Student Exit Outcomes**
*What we want our graduates to be able to do, to be like,
and to know that will directly effect their future success*

**Vision**
*Your mental picture of the future you prefer to create*

---

**Figure 1.4**

The Strategic Alignment box is where "the heavy lifting" begins. In our experiences, we have seen many inspiring and well constructed Strategic Directions that have very little impact on the organization over time. Strategic visions simply don't come to be without strong, dedicated, and courageous leadership. Mass Customized Learning will not come to be without strong, dedicated, passionate, and courageous leadership.

We will learn how important it is to involve people in the change process when we work through the Relational Leader Domain in Chapter 5, but for now, let us make the point that setting the Strategic Direction for a learning community should involve all role groups that have a stake in the most important business in the community. Involvement obviously includes teachers, administrators, and board members . . . but it also includes learners (students), parents, community leaders, the business community, the clergy, law enforcement, etc. Our best Strategic Design results, those with staff and community support, have been with groups of 100 to 120 participants.

*"If it's important, it should be intentional."*
**Stephen Covey**

# LEADERSHIP DOMAINS AND PILLARS OF CHANGE

(cjs) *Bill Spady and I read, studied, and synthesized more than 100 of the most popular "leadership" and "change" books before we created the Total Leaders Framework. We then began asking the question, "What do these 50 or so gurus say that effective leaders actually "DO." Note that the "DO" is in caps to make the point that we looked for behaviors and actions rather than thoughts and theories. We identified fifteen distinctively different activities mentioned frequently in our reading and study that we now call our Total Leader "Performance Roles." Not every guru spoke to all fifteen Performance Roles of course, but we found near unanimous consent within what we came to call our "Leadership Board of Directors," which, we imagined, included: Tom Peters, Daniel Goleman, Margaret Wheatley, Daniel Pink, Chip and Dan Heath. Our board of fifty+ gurus required a large table . . . all wanted to speak at the same time! We think that we were good listeners.*

*A listing of fifteen items is a bit difficult to commit to memory, but with a study of the titles and content of our 100+ bestseller books, we found that the fifteen Performance Roles fit neatly into five one-word categories; sticky words, easy to remember. Those categories became our "Leadership Domains:" Authentic, Visionary, Relational, Quality, Service. The Total Leaders Framework was born. Most of the leadership and change books that you see at Barnes & Noble or at your airport bookstore fit into one or more of the five Leadership Domains. The Total Leaders Framework gets "it" all.*

Refer back to Figures 1.1 and 1.2 as we continue. Total Leaders are:

Authentic Leaders who:
- Create a compelling mission/purpose for the learning community
- Model the learning community's core values and guiding principles
- Are the learning community's lead learner and lead teacher

Visionary Leaders who:
- Define and describe a MCL future for their learning community
- Expand options for the learning community
- Consistently employ a learner focus

Relational Leaders who:
- Develop an open, change-friendly MCL culture
- Involve everyone in the MCL change process
- Create meaning for everyone through the MCL Vision

Quality Leaders who:
- Develop and empower everyone to implement the MCL Vision
- Create and use feedback loops to assess MCL strategies

- Continuously improve the learning community's performance

Service Leaders who:
- Reward positive contributions to the MCL Vision
- Restructure to allow for MCL
- Manage the learning community's MCL Vision

Chapters 3 through 7 will directly apply these five Leadership Domains and fifteen Performance Roles to the implementation of the Inevitable: Mass Customized Learning Vision. We can hardly wait!

## VISION AS REALITY

Right now, the final box on Figure 1.1, *Total Leaders Creating Empowering Change,* may seem to be far off . . . but that IS the target. Do it all and the reward will be a learner-centered learning community where all learners have their learning needs met every hour of every day, where all learners are successful, and where all learners look forward to returning to the learning center early tomorrow.

Today is indeed the opportunity to truly transform education, to bring education into the Information Age, to empower learners for the Age of Empowerment.

## THE MORAL COMPASS OF THE TOTAL LEADER

Total Leaders "know" leadership, and they have the skills to make things happen, but all is for naught if they lack an authentic, value-driven "moral compass." The TL is clear about her "true North" and consistently makes decisions based on personal and core organizational values, and personal and organizational principles of professionalism. What we mean when we use these "moral compass" labels:

- *Personal Values:* Compelling standards of what individuals believe to be right, fair, honorable, important and worthy of consistent attention and action.
- *Core Organizational Values*: Those values that are widely understood, endorsed and consistently acted upon by the organization and by each of its members.
- *Principles of Professionalism:* Those ethical rules of decisions and performances that transcend personal considerations and circumstantial pressures to promote the higher good of the organization and its clients.

# CORE VALUES

Leadership and change literature consistently and continuously identifies old-fashioned core values that never go out of style . . . and we hope that they never do. Our study shows the following core values to be the most honored by leaders who were successful over the long term.

- *Integrity:* The long-term expression and embodiment of honesty, fairness, trustworthiness, honor, and consistent adherence to high-level moral principles, especially those core values and professional principles recognized and endorsed by the organization.
- *Honesty:* Being truthful while being sensitive to the thoughts, needs, and feelings of others.
- *Courage:* The willingness of individuals and organizations to risk themselves despite the likelihood of negative consequences or fear of the unknown.
- *Commitment:* People's willingness to devote their full energies and talents to the successful completion of undertakings they have agreed to pursue, despite challenges and adverse conditions that may arise.
- *Productivity:* The optimum use of available time, resources, technologies, and talent to achieve desired results.

And given today's technology and the fast pace of our world, some (new?) values are now in vogue. Transparency is no longer an option. What you are hiding will eventually be exposed, and just at the wrong time. We now learn more by reflecting on our failures than we do by basking in our successes. Getting there first is important, and you don't get there first without taking chances.

- *Openness:* Is grounded in a sense of psychological security. It reflects a willingness and desire to receive, consider, and act ethically on information, possibilities, and perspectives of all kinds.
- *Reflection:* The process of using a values screen to review, assess, and judge decisions you and your organization have made or will make, and the actions you and your organization have taken or will take.
- *Risk Taking:* Extending beyond the tried, true, and familiar to do different things a different way, often without the assurance of success. Risk taking involves taking initiative, innovating, and speaking out.

# PRINCIPLES OF PROFESSIONALISM

The following Principles of Professionalism are "musts" for the TL. Sometimes it is difficult to distinguish between a core value and a Principle of Professionalism, but that need not be seen as a problem. If it's important, it's important, no matter what we call it! The following five are critical in today's bold leadership and rapidly changing world.

- *Future Focusing:* Conducting a thorough and consistent study of the shifts, trends, and future conditions that redefine a profession, industry, and/or organization, and taking a visionary and far-reaching view of emerging possibilities.
- *Accountability:* Taking responsibility for the content and process of decisions made, actions taken, and the resulting outcomes.
- *Improvement:* A commitment to continuously enhance the quality of personal and organizational performance, the processes used to generate results, and the results themselves.
- *Alignment:* The purposeful, direct matching of decisions, resources, and organizational structures with the organization's declared purpose, vision, and core values.
- *Inclusiveness:* Consistent commitment to maximizing the range of opportunities for success available to organizational members and the number of people included in relevant and meaningful organizational decisions.

This concludes our "short course" on the Total Leaders 2.0 Framework. Chapters 3 through 7 will apply all aspects of this framework to the implementation of the Mass Customized Learning Vision. A reminder . . . the TL 2.0 "complete and unabridged" story is available in book form titled *Total Leaders 2.0: Leading in the Age of Empowerment* by Schwahn and Spady.

# REFLECTION: ASSESS AND PLAN

The following self-assessment rubrics (Figures 1.5 – 1.7) might help you to reflect on your knowledge and skills related to the Total Leaders Framework and to focus your professional development.

**Reflection Question 1 (TL Framework)**

| I. SELF ASSESS<br>(How am I doing?) | What is the degree to which I understand the<br>Total Leaders 2.0 Framework? |
|---|---|
| 4 INNOVATING | *I can lead discussions about the 5 Domains.* |
| 3 APPLYING | *I can identify behaviors / strategies specific to each Domain.* |
| 2 DEVELOPING | *I can define the 5 Domains of the Total Leaders Framework.* |
| 1 BEGINNING | *I can explain why a framework for leadership is important.* |

| II. PLAN FOR IMPROVEMENT<br>(What do I need to do?) | III. SUPPORT RESOURCES<br>(Where can I get help?) |
|---|---|
| *What are strategies that I will do to improve my understanding of the Total Leaders 2.0 Framework?* | *What and / or who are resources that will help me to get better at understanding the Total Leaders 2.0 Framework?* |

**Figure 1.5**

**Reflection Question 2 (TL Framework)**

| I. SELF ASSESS<br>(How am I doing?) | What is the degree to which I understand the<br>components of Strategic Design? |
|---|---|
| 4 INNOVATING | *I can help others understand the components of Strategic Design.* |
| 3 APPLYING | *I can identify the components of Strategic Design that my learning community has done and needs to do.* |
| 2 DEVELOPING | *I can define the components of Strategic Design.* |
| 1 BEGINNING | *I can explain why Strategic Design is important.* |

| II. PLAN FOR IMPROVEMENT<br>(What do I need to do?) | III. SUPPORT RESOURCES<br>(Where can I get help?) |
|---|---|
| *What are strategies that I will do to improve my understanding of Strategic Design?* | *What and / or who are resources that will help me to get better at understanding Strategic Design?* |

**Figure 1.6**

**Reflection Question 3 (TL Framework)**

| I. SELF ASSESS<br>(How am I doing?) | What is the degree to which I have identified my own core values and principles of professionalism that guide how I behave in both my personal and professional lives? |
|---|---|
| 4 INNOVATING | *I am transparent with others about the core values and principles of professionalism that guide my personal and professional lives.* |
| 3 APPLYING | *I have and live by an explicit set of core values and principles of professionalism.* |
| 2 DEVELOPING | *I have an implicit set of core values and principles of professionalism that guide how I live and work.* |
| 1 BEGINNING | *I have not consciously thought about my own core values and principles of professionalism.* |

| II. PLAN FOR IMPROVEMENT<br>(What do I need to do?) | III. SUPPORT RESOURCES<br>(Where can I get help?) |
|---|---|
| *What are strategies that I will do to become more aware of and explicit about the core values and principles of professionalism that guide how I live and work?* | *What and/or who are resources that will help me become more aware of and explicit about the core values and principles of professionalism that guide how I live and work?* |

**Figure 1.7**

Chapter 2

# The Mass Customized
# Learning Vision

*Learning in the Age of*
*Empowerment*

# THE MASS CUSTOMIZED
# LEARNING VISION

### CAN WE SKIP SOMETHINGS?

▶ Education must change . . . significantly!

▶ Many things we used to do made sense . . . they don't anymore!

▶ Technology is here to stay . . . it ~~will~~ is revolutionizing our profession!

▶ Tinkering isn't enough!

## BEING CLEAR FROM THE START

We believe that there is a growing consensus that, although educators work hard and want to be successful, our schools are not serving the needs of our learners or our society very well. The data is out there, and we don't want to rehash it here. We are about placing our energy, and the energy of our fellow educators into transforming schools. We are transforming our schools from their Industrial Age assembly-line structure to an Information Age system that allows for customizing learning for every learner. Technology now makes it possible for schools (or learning communities) to meet the learning needs of every learner, every hour of every day.

The vision described in *Inevitable: Mass Customized Learning . . . Learning in the Age of Empowerment,* has created a buzz, a buzz that continues to get louder. Nearly everyone who reads *Inevitable* wants it! They see the mass customized learning (MCL) vision as highly desirable and most also see it as "doable," not without a good deal of work, but doable. The payoff of a MCL system for our learners mitigates the hard work and the risk involved. Actually, to accept and pursue MCL is much less of a risk than to continue on our present path.

We expect that most people who read this book will already be aware of the *Inevitable: MCL* Vision; they will have read our book and/or attended a conference where the vision was described. But because we want *Inevitable Too! The Total Leader Embraces Mass Customized Learning* to be a stand-alone document, we will highlight the critical aspects of the MCL Vision in this chapter. And because the vision is first, foremost, and continually focused on the learner, we begin with a brief discussion of who that learner is, where she came from, and what her life is like outside of her school experience.

## WHO IS WALKING THROUGH OUR DOORS

We label those born after 1990 as Digital Natives, a phrase first coined by Marc Prensky. They were born digital. They have never experienced anything but a digital world. We think of anyone who remembers IBM typewriters, white out, letters typed and sent via the US mail, news at 5:30 PM, telephone cords, handwritten receipts, and athletes who didn't gloat, as Digital Immigrants. Now to be fair, we quickly admit that there are many Digital Immigrants who have learned that second language, but for most of us, it has been a rather long and relatively flat learning curve . . . and we still speak with a bit of an accent. Digital is the Digital Natives' first language. Did little Bobby say "iPad" or "Mommy" first?

The technology of the last decade has changed everything. Now that statement might be too strong, but we think that it is more accurate than to say it "changed many or most things." Technology has shifted a good deal of power from the Digital Immigrants to the Digital Natives. We have moved from "Father Knows Best" to "Hey Bobby, can you help me to find that financial webpage or whatever they call it;" from "Now where did I put that chicken enchilada recipe," to "Just a second, Mom, I'll Google it for you."

So who is this learner walking through our door, what have been his experiences, how does he learn, how does he manage his world? We offer some points about today's DNs that help us paint a portrait.

- Digits have always been part of the DN's environment. Ho Hum!
- DNs learned to manipulate technology early and have never been afraid of it. They haven't had to relearn anything. Having to use "white out" if they make a mistake is not a threat.
- There has been a bit of a role reversal regarding things digital . . . DNs are frequently their parents' teachers . . . and on occasion, their teachers' teachers.

- DNs are controlling markets and their cultural environment. The world is listening to them and giving them what they want.
- DNs expect interaction; they no longer accept one-way broadcasts. They are not only consumers of information; they are also creators of information.
- DNs are probably smarter and savvier than previous generations. (Now don't take that personally. You too are probably guilty of telling everyone how intelligent your grandkids are and how they manage the computer with ease. We plead guilty!)
- DNs think about the world differently. Their solutions are different, and their work environments are totally different.
- DNs will transform organizations, politics . . . and, inevitably, education.
- On the downside, the issue of privacy is the #1 concern of adult digital experts . . . but not the concern of many DNs.

The point here is to identify and accept how today's learners differ from yesterday's students. They have different backgrounds, different experiences, different expectations, and different needs. What we taught and how we taught in the past no longer works very well. If nothing else in our world had changed, would the "different kid" who walks through our door create a powerful need for changing how we do school? We think that the answer to that question is an obvious "yes."

We actually believe that to continue to call the boys and girls, the young men and women who walk through our doors "students" is an inaccurate and outdated label. Instead, those walking through our doors are "learners," learners who have always lived in the Age of Empowerment. We must treat them as empowered learners if we want motivated, self-directed learners who are in the process of becoming life-long learners.

> *"When you visit high schools, it's striking to note the difference in affect and energy between hallways and classrooms. Boredom may be the greatest challenge we face."*
>
> **Getting Smart: How Digital Learning Is Changing the World**
>
> **Tom Vander Ark**

# AMAZON KNOWS ME LIKE A BOOK

*(cjs) iTunes Genius knows that I like Waylon and Willie and seldom recommends Mozart. Amazon knows that I like books about leadership and the future. Google understands my*

*question in four or five key strokes . . . almost as quickly as my bride. Visa knows within two or three purchases if someone might have stolen my card.*

*On the other hand, the USPS makes me wait in line and doesn't remember or care that I mail a lot of books. The DMV doesn't care that I never take my black '90 F150 on the highway; I still have to license "Zorro" and pay for the roads that it will not be driven on. The policies of the State Department of Education <u>still</u> require seat time and credit hours to credential student learning; competency is merely a second thought or not thought of at all.*

The first paragraph of this section is about "customer/client-centered" organizations. The second is about bureaucracies that are designed for "administrative convenience." Call the question:

*In which paragraph does the Industrial Age, assembly-line school fit today?*

Where *should* schools fit? Should we educators make decisions with an "administratively convenient" mindset, or should we be customer/client/learner-centered when we organize our system and interact with our learners? The customer focused organizations in the first paragraph are "mass customizing" their services. The bureaucratic organizations in the second paragraph are "mass producing" their services.

The impact of the Information Age did not change the products and services we receive. It changed how we receive them AND who is in control. Many miss that when the "Age" shifted, so did the power. We moved from organizations and businesses being in control to customers and clients in control. Purchasers and users of products and services are now telling organizations and businesses what they want, what they will pay for it, and how they expect to be treated throughout the purchasing and using experience. With the Information Age came the Age of Empowerment. Are there any implications for education and learners???

---

The Industrial Age gave us
MASS PRODUCTION

The Information Age gave us
MASS CUSTOMIZATION

which in turn made

The Age of Empowerment
INEVITABLE

---

**Figure 2.1**

**Mass Customization defined:** The capacity to routinely customize products and services to meet the specific needs and/or desires of individuals while simultaneously meeting the specific needs of other individuals . . . and all of this without adding significantly to the cost of the product or service.

**Mass Customized Learning defined:** Meeting the personal learning needs of individual learners every hour of every day, while simultaneously meeting the personal learning needs of all other learners every hour of every day.

We couldn't have done this 10 years ago.. The technology to do so was not available. It is available today as proven by the large number of businesses/organizations that today are routinely "mass customizing" their products and services. Think Starbucks where you can routinely order a hot venti chai, no fat, no foam, no water, and extra hot, while the person behind you asks for a large coffee . . . "with a little room."

The vision or ability to customize learning is hiding in plain sight. Cross-industry borrowing is how other businesses and industries innovate. They *see* concepts and ideas that are working in other industries that they borrow and adjust to their industry. We in education are poised to do the same.

When you experience a customized service – from iTunes, from Amazon, from Google, from United Airlines, from a shopping site, ask yourself two (rhetorical) questions:

1. How do they DO that?
2. Are there any implications for education?

It is our strong opinion that MASS CUSTOMIZED LEARNING has the power to move public education from a bureaucratic industry to an effective and efficient profession. Teachers should and will embrace that opportunity. Being a professional requires that we apply our best and most basic research. Our present assembly-line organizational structure doesn't encourage, nor allow, teachers to act on individual learning needs, respond to individual learning styles, or to teach a concept or a skill using content of interest to that learner. Until we are able to meet learners at their personal need level in these three basic categories, it is difficult to think of our work as a profession.

Figure 2.2 presents a sharp contrast between the Industrial Age and the Information Age. The distinction here is with learning opportunities, rigidity compared to flexibility. The contrast is great. And, the impact that technology will have on education and learning is only in its infancy.

**From RIGIDITY to FLEXIBILITY**

| INDUSTRIAL AGE Paradigm of "School" | INFORMATION AGE Paradigm of "Learning Systems" |
|:---:|:---:|
| Specific Students | Anyone |
| *can learn* | *can learn* |
| Specific Subjects | Anything |
| *in* | *from* |
| Specific Classrooms | Anywhere |
| *on a* | *at* |
| Specific Schedule | Any time |
| *in a* | *in* |
| Specific Way | Any Way |
| *from a* | *from* |
| Specific Teacher | World Wide Experts |

**Figure 2.2**

The Information Age didn't change WHAT services and products we received. It changed HOW we received them. For example, the Industrial Age gave us garage sales; the Information Age gave us eBay. I *still* buy other people's junk and call it a treasure. How I do it has changed. Learners will still learn the curriculum. They will *still* learn to read, to write, to calculate, to think and apply. How they experience learning will look different. More on this later . . .

## "DON'T THROW OUT THE BABY WITH THE BATHWATER"

We hear that statement often, usually said in defense of the status quo. We agree. There are time-honored strategies, many taught to us by Madeline Hunter, that are still effective. The real question is:

*"So, what is baby and what is bathwater?"*

Figure 2.3 helps to answer that question.

| **BABY** *Those practices that have their roots in:* | **BATHWATER** *Those practices and strategies that are based on:* |
|:---:|:---:|
| RESEARCH | TRADITION |
| ACCEPTED THEORY | NORMS |
| EXPERT OPINION | CONVENIENCE |
| SUCCESSFUL EXPERIENCES | HABIT |

**Figure 2.3**

So what about schools and how we do things today is "baby," and what is "bathwater?"

Those old enough to remember the "wash tub" being the "bath tub" will know that although you don't throw the baby out with the bathwater, you also don't throw the bathwater out just because it's bathwater. Bathwater is thrown out when there is cleaner and warmer bathwater available. The Industrial Age bathwater is both cold and rather dirty. MCL is that cleaner and warmer bathwater that allows us to act on our "babies," those things about learning and learners that are tried and true.

Our Top Ten "Babies," all of which fit neatly into the MCL Vision:

1.  Learning rates vary and prior knowledge is significant to learning new knowledge.
2.  Motivation spikes with learner interest.
3.  Learning styles differ and intelligence is multi-dimensional.
4.  Success breeds success and influences esteem, attitude, and motivation.
5.  Mistakes are inherent in the learning process and specific feedback enhances learning.
6.  Requisite complex reasoning skills can be taught/learned.
7.  Real world contexts/problems enhance learning.
8.  Learning is social.
9.  Technology can be "teacher" for many learner outcomes.
10. Schools/teachers control the conditions for learner success.

And a few "bathwaters," none of which are part of the MCL Vision:

1. Grade Levels
2. Students Permanently Assigned to Specific Classrooms
3. Class Periods/Bell Schedules
4. Textbooks
5. ABC Grading
6. Report Cards
7. Learning Happens in School
8. Nine-Month School Year

# THE SECONDARY SCHOOL STRUCTURE

*Inevitable: MCL* is a vision . . . . a vision that is rather quickly becoming a reality in a number of school systems throughout the United States. Describing the vision in a present tense rather than a future tense makes it more motivating, concrete, and powerful. There are three ways you can experience our description of what the MCL Vision would look like at the secondary level:

- Read or re-read Chapter 7 in *Inevitable: Mass Customized Learning.*
- Watch the video, *MCL: Lori Schedules Her Learning Plan.* You can access it at www.masscustomizedlearning.com or on YouTube. Search "MCL: Lori Schedules Her Learning Plan."
- Read the following abbreviated description.

When you experience Lori doing her schedule, you will come to know and feel how desirable and doable the MCL Vision is. You will want it for YOUR children, our learners, our profession, and for our society.

The MCL Vision feels quite real when Lori does her Learning Plan. Fourteen-year-old Lori is doing her two month Learning Plan with her father. Depending on the learner's self-directedness and his parent's involvement, a Learning Coach may be more directive in creating the learner's Learning Plan. This scene, whether with a parent or a Learning Coach, will become a reality in school systems in the near future; MCL is, after all, "Inevitable."

For those of you new to MCL, we will describe the process to the point that you will get the feel of a learner being responsible for her own learning AND what it takes for a system to make Lori's learning experiences a reality.

## LORI'S SCHEDULING SEQUENCE

The scheduling sequence listed in Figure 2.4 guides Lori through her scheduling process. Lori attends a Learning Center named Lincoln Unlimited Learning Center (LULC), and Ms. Trezona is her Learning Coach. Lori is creating her schedule on her iPad.

Lori's Scheduling Sequence
*from the least flexible to the most flexible*

1. Team Sports and Music (e.g. Gymnastics and Band)
2. Seminars (e.g. Interpersonal Communications)
3. Group Learning Online (e.g. Math online learning w/three friends)
4. Laboratories (e.g. Science)
5. Personal Interests (e.g. Economics of the Music World)
6. Personal Learning Online (e.g. Math/U.S. History)

**Figure 2.4**

Lori introduces herself to you: *I am working through my learning program at Lincoln Unlimited Learning Center. The LULC serves about 4,000 learners from four- and five-year-old preschoolers to 17- and 18-year-olds who are completing their programs. Our schools have changed significantly over the past few years. Five years ago the community went through a future-focused planning process that resulted in a school name change and a new way of scheduling our learning activities. Today we all have individual learning plans, and based on our past behavior and accomplishments, my friends and I have a lot to say about our learning schedule.*

*I am doing my schedule for the first two months, and I will explain what I am doing and why I am doing it. There are a few learners in our learning community who have their schedules planned for them, but most everyone has gradually learned to do their own planning as they progress through their learner outcomes. We are the only school system in our area that is doing* MASS CUSTOMIZED LEARNING *but we are getting many visitors who want to learn about how our learning community operates.*

*MCL works well for my friends and me. We go through the learner outcomes at our own pace and most of the graduates of LULC are well ahead of those who graduated from the old program that moved everyone along at the same pace.*

---

*Today is August 1 and I will be planning my schedule for September and October. I have found it best to schedule my learning activities in advance so that I can get into the seminars I want and my friends and I can coordinate our activities. I like to stay at least one month ahead with my schedule.*

*I talk with my Mom and Dad about my schedule all the time and they make suggestions as to what I should do . . . actually, they probably have veto power but it never seems to come to that. Ms. Trezona is my Learning Coach and she definitely has veto power over my schedule. Ms. Trezona knows me well. She has coached me for the past two years and I actually got to pick her to be my coach. She is a tough cookie with high expectations and I actually like her for that!*

*Today I am doing my schedule with my Dad. I pretty well know what I will do but Dad wants to be involved and sometimes he has pretty good ideas. Ms. Trezona does not think that she has to be involved in planning my schedule, but she will review it and respond soon after I hit "send."*

*Step 1 is for me to review my learning portfolio. What learner outcomes have I completed and which outcomes should I be attending to next? All LULC learner outcomes matched to my electronic learning portfolio are available online from the LULC web page.*

---

The System's Work (in order for Lori and all learners to create a customized Learning Plan):

1.  The leaders of LULC completed a Strategic Design process that identified the exit learner outcomes for their graduates. Not a simple task, but one that is meaningful and doable.

2.  The Curriculum and Instruction people of the organization . . .with input from ~~teachers~~ Learning Facilitators of course . . . worked back from the exit learner outcomes to create enabling outcomes for all levels of learning. Not a simple task, but one that is necessary and doable.

3.  The Information Technology people . . . with input from the curriculum and instruction people and Learning Facilitators of course . . . created an electronic portfolio system that automatically documents the learner performances that are required for proof of learner mastery. Not an easy task but one that has been accomplished by some learning systems.

> Lori continues: *With some coaching from Ms. Trezona, I have learned that there is a planning sequence that saves me from having to make major revisions just when I think that I am about finished with my schedule. The tip: first schedule those activities that are the least flexible and cannot be easily changed, and save the flexible stuff for the end. I love gymnastics, I do all-around, and I compete for the LULC gymnastics team. Gymnastics is my most rigidly scheduled activity so I will schedule it first. Practice is from 3:30 to 5:00 Monday through Friday except for the days when we have meets scheduled. It's a simple process to schedule my practices and my meets when most of my days are blank.*

The System's Work:

1. LULC creates and publishes an annual online calendar of events that includes everything learners will have to know to create their personal schedules. The calendar includes all scheduled gymnastics meets.

2. The system has adopted the Microsoft Exchange Calendar throughout the system. (They could have chosen a scheduling calendar from a number of competing companies, but designating one specific calendar makes the integration of calendars more friction free.)

3. Lori's schedule is made available to anyone "with a need to know" . . . and those with a need to know will have a password that ensures privacy. Lori, her parents, her Learning Coach, and the LULC principal are designated as people "with a need to know."

> Lori continues: *The next least flexible type of learning activity at LULC is the in-depth seminars that are designed around complex learner outcomes that require interaction between the learning facilitator and me and between my classmates and me. I want to schedule:*
>
> - *the Interpersonal Communications seminar (a 30-hour commitment)*
>
> - *the Diversity seminar (a 24-hour commitment) and*
>
> - *the Creating and Defending a Business Plan seminar (a 27-hour commitment)*
>
> *After thinking it over, I think that I could also complete*
>
> - *the Forms of Government seminar (a 20-hour commitment)*
>
> *during the next 60 days . . . it will crowd my calendar a bit but three of my friends are scheduling it too.*

*Each of the four seminars I want to take is scheduled at least once during September and October. I will schedule those that are only offered once first and hope that I get them . . . you can see now why I like to do my scheduling at least a month before the activity is to happen. If I can't get the seminars I want when I want them because they are filled, I will schedule them the next time they are offered so I can be sure to complete them sometime soon. Or, the Learning Facilitators often create additional sections of a seminar when there is interest. Well here goes, wish me luck . . . and wish my friends luck too because we are trying to get into the same seminars.*

The System's Work:

1.  The curriculum and instruction people . . . with input from Learning Facilitators of course . . . went through all of the LULC learner outcomes and answered the following question for each of them, "How is this learner outcome best learned?" A **most important question!**

2.  For those learner outcomes best learned online with a computer, they identified or created online learning opportunities. These online learning activities, including a built-in learner assessment, were made available on the LULC web page 24/7.

3.  For those learner outcomes best learned in a seminar format, the curriculum and instruction people . . . with much input from specific Learning Facilitators of course . . . developed seminars much like colleges and universities create, describe, and schedule courses. Each seminar topic can be directly traced to an exit learner outcome and to one or more Spheres of Living from the Strategic Design planning process.

4.  The online seminar-scheduling program is coordinated with the individual learner's scheduling process. If the Interpersonal Communications seminar only accommodates 18 learners and it has been filled, anyone attempting to schedule that seminar will be informed that the seminar is filled and informed of other available dates with openings. Or, the Learning Facilitators (teachers) determine that an additional section of that seminar is needed and who will lead that seminar. This is the school readying itself for the learners versus the learners fitting into a fixed schedule of seminars.

Lori continues: *Much of my Science is online . . . even many of my experiments are conducted via virtual reality. But there are things that our Science Learning Facilitators want done in the Science lab and I enjoy that. It gives me a chance to meet other learners and to actually touch things. Scheduling my Science lab time is usually quite easy. Scheduling lab time seems to be more flexible than*

---

*scheduling seminars. So after I have my seminars scheduled I block out times to be in the Science lab.*

*Some of the lab work requires preparation, so when I get to a certain place in my online learning outcomes I am automatically informed of when that lab experience will be offered. I look for empty spaces in my schedule and schedule lab times at times and places that are easy to coordinate with my other activities of the day. After doing my schedule for a couple of years I have learned how to save time and travel.*

---

The System's Work:

1. Virtual reality has made it possible to conduct many experiments online. But for those learning activities requiring labs and other hands-on experiences, the curriculum and instruction people . . . with input from specific Learning Facilitators of course . . . create, describe, and schedule activities much like Science labs in high schools and universities and much like our best Technical Training Institutes. These hands-on learning experiences can be scheduled much like the seminars described above except that the location of the learning activity, by its nature, must be more site specific.

2. Seminar and lab attendance is monitored. Attendance is taken at all sessions and parents are automatically contacted and informed about a learner absence. Learning Community leaders know where each student is to be at any time of the day. Their name or number is entered into the master schedule program, which instantly brings up their daily schedule including activities and locations.

---

Lori continues: *Doing online learning by yourself makes it easy to schedule . . . I am the only one I need to be concerned about, but it can be a bit boring after awhile. I have three good friends . . . all girls with whom I do my online Math. We all are at about the same place in Math and we go at about the same speed. We have fun of course and we help each other when one of us needs some quick tutoring. We set aside 6 to 8 hours each week to work together on Math . . . we find a time that fits into all of our schedules by using our Microsoft scheduling calendars to automatically find times when all four of us are free. Sometimes we do our work in the Learning Center computer lab and sometimes we meet in one of our homes. We live close to each other and often coordinate our travel time. Everyone at LULC has a laptop and access to the Internet of course.*

---

The System's Work:

1. The Microsoft Exchange Calendar makes it possible to coordinate the personal calendars. This technology is also available from many other IT companies. The LULC would have to make that service available to all staff and all learners.

---

Lori continues: *The LULC is very good about meeting my learning needs, but there are some things that I want to learn and want to do that don't fit into the MCL program. When I have something that I want to do and don't know how to go about it, I schedule a time to discuss it with Ms. Trezona. For instance, because I have an interest in music and want to learn how businesses work, I would like to do a project that would help me to learn about how the music business works. I doubt that I will ever be an entertainer, but I think that I might be interested in a career in the business side of the music industry.*

*My Mom has a friend who works at a bank who used to be a professional entertainer in the pop music field. I have talked with Mom's friend and she seemed excited to think that she might mentor me in my study of the music industry . . . her banking experience would help with the financial part of the industry and she too was looking forward to learning more about what I wanted to learn about.*

*One of our learner outcomes from the Economic Sphere of Living is about business plans. Although the LULC has a seminar on that outcome I am allowed to do a personal project in place of that seminar as long as I can demonstrate the learner outcomes. Ms. Trezona has the authority to OK that project for me and she has agreed to facilitate a planning meeting between my mentor and me. I am really excited about it; who knows, one day I might be a talent scout! I have a friend who is thinking about joining me in this project. Christopher is interested in this topic too.*

---

The System's Work:

1. The key to this type of flexibility lies in writing learner outcomes that are demonstrations of learning. That is, outcomes that are clear about what the learner must do to demonstrate mastery of that learning outcome. Traditional curriculum tends to be about "topics, about what the course will cover."

2. This type of flexibility will be difficult to find in school systems that do not have a learner-centered, outcome based, open and flexible culture. Creating that culture is everyone's responsibility but it must involve and begin with the system's leaders.

3. We frequently hear phrases like "the community is our school" which usually means that people volunteer to help out in classrooms. A good thing, but

that's not what we are suggesting here. A real Learning Community goes far beyond that and it does it intentionally and systematically. Economic seminars take place at the bank and bank directors facilitate; biology seminars take place in hospitals and are facilitated by doctors and nurses; and mentors from all professions and occupations are eager to coach a young learner through a meaningful and real project.

---

Lori continues: *The last thing I put on my learning calendar is the online outcomes that I do by myself and can schedule at my convenience. Mom and Dad think that it is best if I schedule my days much like someone with a regular job would do, which means a minimum of a 40-hour week. I carry my iPad wherever I go, and so I can work on my online learner outcomes whenever I have the time . . . but I do schedule them in advance to stop me from getting lazy.*

*I can also work on the online outcomes from anywhere, which helps a lot with my schedule. My preference is to work on them at home but I find that many times I have gaps in my schedule when it would be difficult and time consuming to get home and then back to another activity. So most of the time I just try to find a quiet place, get out my iPad, call up my learner portfolio and go for it. Our Learning Community has many places where we can work online. Even businesses seem to like to see us working in their places. Internet hotspots are everywhere . . . wish I could afford Starbucks more often.*

*My friends and I have become a little competitive about our progress. I think that my three girlfriends and I will complete all of the exit learner outcomes and be eligible for graduation before we are seventeen. That is our target anyway.*

---

The System's Work:

1. Earlier we described what the Learning Community must do to make their online learning activities available for learners 24/7. Selecting or creating, organizing, testing, and making online learning activities available is a large task and must be one of the first projects initiated soon after a MCL Vision has been agreed upon. The good news is that there are already good programs available and more are being created all the time. Learning Communities, educators, and learners will soon have alternatives for most learner outcomes that are common to curriculum. Today's digital world has made choice ubiquitous.

2. Credit card companies have programs to determine the amount customers must pay on their account each month and customers are contacted . . . and probably threatened if the minimum amount is not paid. Wal-Mart has

a computerized system to know exactly when one of their products must be ordered to ensure that the product will continue to be available to customers. That type of technology could easily be used to determine when individual learners are falling behind on their online learner outcomes. Learning systems will want to implement a feedback loop that will automatically inform "those with a need to know," including parents of course, when a learner is not meeting expectations. They will also want to inform the "need to knowers" when a learner is exceeding expectations. And the acceptable rates of progress can differ for learners. Not all learners learn at the same rate. The danger will be in having lower expectations for some learners simply because of their socio-economic status or some other indefensible criterion.

---

Lori continues: *So there it is, my learning schedule for September and October. You can see everything that I hope to accomplish these two months. My Dad has given it an OK and I will now hit "send" and it will go to Ms. Trezona, my Learning Coach, my Mom and Dad's inbox, my gymnastics coach, all of the seminar and lab Learning Facilitators whose learning activities I have scheduled, and to the Learning Community Central Office. The only one on my list who may want me to make a change in my schedule will be Ms. Trezona, and she always gets back to me right away if she thinks I should make a change.*

*My parents, who refer to themselves as "digital immigrants," are afraid that I might depend on the computer and the Internet too much, and that I won't have enough opportunities to interact and work with other kids. So Dad and I always do a check of my learning plan to see if we can keep it about 50 – 50. It doesn't have to be exact but he wants me to have about the same amount of time with group experiences as with individual online learning.*

---

## LETTING FAST RUNNERS RUN

You may think that Lori is an exceptional kid and that there aren't many like her, but in our experiences as teachers and principals, there are a lot of Loris out there who only need to have the ceiling on learning removed so they can excel far beyond what they now are allowed and encouraged to do. We confidently estimate that if MCL were a reality for our learners, far more than 50% of our students would outdistance what the top 5% now accomplish. When we combine the learner motivation that is fostered by MCL with the tools to learn that encourage rather than impede acceleration, test scores are sure to rise significantly. And a love for learning is retained.

And none of this is at the expense of the slower learner. The slower runner runs faster than we ever expected! They too will have their daily learning needs met without the stigma of being in a special program. They too would most likely see their motivation and achievement increase. Although we believe that today's schools place too much emphasis on high-stakes testing, we believe that composite test scores in the United States would increase to the point that we would again lead the world in learner achievement. The potential of MCL is great.

A Little Story *(bmcg)When Chuck and I wrote Inevitable, we debated using the phrases "fast runners" and "slow runners." I was worried. Would these phrases cement "bell-curve thinking?" Chuck, as many of you know, is very persuasive. So . . . the phrases remained. Months after the book was published, I was invited to a Grade 4 classroom in Maine. The teacher wanted me to see her mass customized learning classroom, to experience the growth mindset culture she had created.*

*My visit will always be memorable and special. Her learners inundated me with stories of their successes! Imbedded in their stories were phrases such as "going at my own pace," "my style of learning," "With effort and teacher help, I can now . . ." And then I heard, "I'm a fast runner on . . . I'm a slow runner on . . ." My internal alarm went off. Damn! I don't want them to label themselves as such. I <u>knew</u> this would happen! It negates all that Carol Dweck has taught us about fixed and growth mindset thinking!*

*Needing clarification, I asked them, speaking directly to one little guy. "So, Josh, you said you're a 'slow runner' on writing paragraphs. You're just not good at writing paragraphs?" His look was strange — almost incredulous — and said — slowly, as if wondering if I had read my own book, "Well, not right now, but I WILL get better at it. I will be a fast runner at it eventually. You see . . ." And, he went on to describe, as did others, how they each are good at some things and need work on other things. No big deal! And, with peer and teacher help, they become — well — fast runners.*

# THE ELEMENTARY & MIDDLE SCHOOL STRUCTURE

When we wrote and published *Inevitable*, our major concern was with the time-based, limiting Industrial Age structure of our secondary schools. It still is! But we quickly began to receive questions about how we would apply the MCL Vision to the elementary school. That feedback motivated us to add a chapter to *Inevitable* that describes our vision of a flexible and effective structure for elementary learners, teachers, and schools. The entire Elementary MCL Vision chapter is available at the masscustomizedlearning.com website. Give it a study if you want to know more.

Our vision for a MCL elementary and middle school structure differs significantly from the structure of our ideal high school. High schools are structured as one comprehensive and complex organization. When one part of the HS master schedule is changed, it can, and usually does, impact many other aspects of the schedule. The structure of the typical elementary or middle school is not nearly as tightly aligned. One teacher, or a teaching team, can modify their schedule quite freely without impacting any other classrooms. As we thought about the MCL Elementary Vision, we recalled what we learned from Dr. Madeline Hunter. Let's reminisce a bit . . .

## CHANNELING MADELINE

Dr. Madeline Hunter, UCLA professor and principal of the UCLA Lab School was our heroine in the late '60s. Her knowledge about learning and her passion for learners made us disciples of her beliefs, theories, and research. Dr. Hunter organized and structured the UCLA lab school around three complementary innovations that she and her staff implemented simultaneously.

Dr. Hunter knew, and believed, that all 6 year-olds did NOT have the same learning needs, and therefore, to put all 6 year-olds together in a 1$^{st}$ grade classroom with one teacher, simply because of their age, didn't make sense. Dr. Hunter believed that elementary schools should be **NON-GRADED**.

*A Little Story (cjs): I heard Dr. Hunter speak to groups of educators a number of times. I got to know her well. She usually took questions. After one of her presentations a teacher asked, "At what age do you think children are ready for kindergarten?" Dr. Hunter responded thoughtfully and softly (and she was always "cool"), "I think that is the wrong question. The real question is 'What is that child ready for?'" It was a brief dialogue that had a lasting impact. Dr. Hunter was a learner-centered person, and her response was a learner-centered response. I learned that day what it meant to be learner-centered. She changed how I think about putting first things first.*

Dr. Hunter knew and believed that three or four teachers teaming would offer more learning opportunities for learners. She also believed that teachers would become more professional as they studied, learned, and taught together. And therefore, Dr. Hunter believed that the school should be organized around teaching teams; she labeled it **TEAM TEACHING.**

Dr. Hunter knew and believed that teaching teams could be more efficient and more learner-centered in their grouping if they were grouping learners based on their learning needs not by age or ability. She also believed that older children could provide positive role models for the younger learners. She believed that school would be a richer experience for learners if they were non-graded, team-taught, and **MULTI-AGED.**

Elementary non-graded, multi-age teams have existed since Dr. Hunter's time. Hard working, dedicated, and talented teachers have tried to provide rich learning opportunities for children, *but it hasn't been easy.* Today it still isn't easy, but technology has made the non-graded, multi-age team more efficient and effective. Technology, especially when it includes electronic learning portfolios, can also help teaching teams manage their grouping and regrouping process.

You will see Dr. Hunter's themes of *non-graded, multi-age groupings*, and *team teaching* throughout the MCL Elementary/Middle School Vision — with a twist of technology.

## FORM FOLLOWS FUNCTION

This phrase, "form follows function," with its architectural roots helped us to envision a learning community at the elementary or middle level. Instead of putting a new coat of paint on the current structure or form of school, we thought first of the function or purpose of a learning community.

Rather than to be very specific about how a MCL elementary/middle school should be structured (the form), we began with guidelines (the function) that will help teams of teachers create a structure that meets the needs of their specific team and their specific learners. When we created the MCL HS Vision, we were thinking of 1500 learners and approximately 60 teachers. As we created this MCL Elementary School Vision, we were thinking of an elementary or middle school of 400 to 600 learners. A good place to start is with approximately 75-100 multi-age learners and 3 or 4 teachers — teams of learning facilitators. An expanded option might include more learning facilitators all focusing on specific learning goals within a content area. The more learning facilitators, the more they can "share the load."

Therefore, we are quite firm with "guidelines" that are core to the vision, and a bit less directive with how it might look. We will share, in a bit, some "best options" being designed by teams of learning facilitators.

But, first let's take a look at our firm guidelines for the Elementary/Middle School MCL Vision. When we visit classrooms in learning communities, we watch for three firm guidelines:

1. Learning facilitators (teachers) sharing the load;
2. Flexible grouping and regrouping of learners around specific learning goals; not tracking (!);
3. Learners invested in their learning.

# GUIDELINE # 1: SHARING THE LOAD

It is impossible for a single teacher in a single classroom to meet the learning needs of every learner every day. There. We said it. A requisite for mass customizing learning is for learning facilitators to *share the load*.

Instead of every learning facilitator being responsible for and expert in every single learning goal or topic, they become the expert or "guru" in specific areas for the learning community. Their moniker is "Fraction Guru" or "Narrative Writing Guru" instead of "Grade 4 Teacher." This sharing capitalizes on the strengths and interests of the learning facilitators. <u>And</u>, the Fraction Guru can more easily differentiate to meet the individual learning needs of each learner. Another learning facilitator is doing the same for, let's say, narrative writing.

*Meeting the individual needs of learners* means creating learning opportunities for those fraction related learner outcomes based on:

the learning level of the learner;
the learning style of the learner;
the interests of the learner; and
the relevance of the learning to the learner's world.

Much easier to do if learning facilitators are sharing the load! Additionally, meeting the needs of individual learners would involve identifying those fraction related learner outcomes best learned online.

> *"How does the virtual learning experience*
> *SUPERCHARGE*
> *what happens inside*
> *the physical learning experience?"*
>
> **Salman Kahn**

We expect that approximately 30% - 40% of elementary learner outcomes – the simpler, more literal learning goals - could be learned online effectively and efficiently, leaving teachers with smaller groups and allowing for personalized learning around the complex learning goals. Salman Kahn's quote says it. We want to be clear. Technology will not replace teachers. Learners need teachers. Key questions for the Fraction Guru are "What are those fraction related outcomes that are best learned online? And, what are those that require face-to-face experiences with the learning facilitator?" Let's outsource what we can to technology freeing the learning facilitator to focus on those complex application and problem solving goals.

# GUIDELINE # 2: GROUPING AND REGROUPING

Non-grading, multi-age grouping, and team teaching can be observed. On a visit, we see these structures in operation, hear the buzz, and see learners engaged in differing activities. But the thing we don't see, and can't see, is, "How did these kids get to these specific groups, to these specific learning opportunities; how do they know where to go; what criteria did learning facilitators use to form these groups; in the end, how will we know that kids aren't falling through the cracks . . ."

Because these concerns are so critical to the "would-be adopter" of the Elementary MCL Vision, we share with you four levels of how learning facilitators might design for MCL. In the spirit of being transparent, know that the names of these learning facilitators are fictitious and their stories are composites of what some teams are doing or planning to do.

## THE POWER GOAL MODEL (Michelle's Story)

*I'm Michelle. I am a member of a three person team working with 75 learners ages 6-8.*

*When visitors come to our school to see our MCL team in operation, they always ask us how we group our kids, why are these learners in this particular group, how do the children know where to go, do these groups change or are they like the "blackbirds, redbirds, and bluebirds." In a way, the process we use for grouping is very complex. We are beginning to use electronic portfolio software to help us keep track of the learning goals for each learner and this helps us to form groups. But in another way, a more practical way, the grouping process our team first used was quite simple.*

*We began by forming cross grade level teams. Some teams in our Learning Community cross two grade levels. Others cross three grade levels. It used to make sense to group learners according to age . . . or did it ever? Now, it makes more sense to share the load as Learning Facilitators. We realized there were 6-, 7-, and 8-year olds that had the same learning need, for instance, adding two digits. Why weren't we sharing the load to address* this learning need? Some learners needed place value, while others needed to understand measurement. Thus began what we now term our "Power Goal Sessions."

Every once in a while, the three of us Learning Facilitators would say, it is time . . . Time to schedule a one to two week focus on "power goals." We would identify three learnings that our learners needed. Jokingly, we asked, "What are the three things that are driving us to eat a bag of M & M peanuts every night," as we lament what these kids still don't know! Three — because there were three of us. Sometimes we were able to include the Assistant Principal, which gave us a fourth goal. We started with Math because it seemed the easiest due to its hierarchical nature.

Once the goals were identified, we sorted which learner needed which power goal. Before our technology software was up and running, we did this ourselves. It wasn't hard to do so. I only had to look at my 28 learners and determine which of the four power goals would be their focus. And so . . . we grouped them. Notice, everyone has a power goal. This is not about creating an "intervention" period. As well intended as that is, it not so subtly creates what Carol Dweck (Mindset: The New Psychology of Success) would call a fixed mindset culture.

Let me take a minute to describe how the learning would happen within the Power Goal class. When I was the Fraction Power Goal teacher, I would have 2-4 sub-groups or levels of fractions within the class. We came to affectionately call them: Baby-bear fractions; Momma-bear fractions; Papa-bear fractions; and sometimes Grampy-fractions. We designed these groups similar to what used to be called "centers." These power goal centers included independent work, partner work, and technology supported work. Periodically, each group would meet me at my teaching table for direct instruction from me . . . 'cause they need me! Notice that it was easy for me to design, differentiate, and customize the center work for individuals because I only had fractions to worry about. I was able to design activities and strategies for specific learning styles and learning interests. This was SO freeing and empowering!

The key — and this is important to MCL — the Baby-bear fraction learners did not move as a cohort to the next level. Instead, learners could move at their own pace. A learner — a fast runner — could zoom through a couple levels in a short period of time.

The result was quite amazing! Our learners were engaged — meeting with success. That old adage, "Success breeds success," became our refrain. And . . . because of how we structured or re-structured we were able to laser the instruction — customize it to those groups of learners. Because we were able to efficiently focus our instruction, they became proficient. The more proficient they became the more engaged they were. The more engaged they were, the more proficient they became. Hard to tell which came first the chicken or the egg . . . the success or the engagement!

We also added a tracking component. Some teams used the concept of Merit Badge; others the concept of Passport Book. As learners demonstrated mastery for — let's say — Baby-bear fractions, their Passport Book was stamped or they received a quarter of their Merit

*would not have motivated (pushed?) us to think differently. But together they caused significant tension and disequilibrium. We finally accepted and faced the following realities:*

▶ *More and more learners were not meeting with success.*

▶ *No longer could we rationalize failure, as "That's just the way it is. Some are smart and some are not."*

▶ *Bless our hearts . . . we have tried to meet the individual needs of kids, but it is ~~nearly~~ impossible to do it alone.*

▶ *MCL is the vision we have always had and wanted. MCL brings hope.*

*And so . . . our "Team Five" rolled up our sleeves to significantly change how we delivered the learning. We began by reading three books:*

*Inevitable: Mass Customized Learning (Schwahn & McGarvey)*
*Mindset (Dweck)*
*The One World Schoolhouse (Kahn)*

*We were motivated by the video of Chapter 7 in Inevitable and thought, "How could we do that for little guys?" Thus began our creating "The Seminar Model."*

*As with most Learning Facilitators, we are overwhelmed with the number of standards and benchmarks expected of learners. There are way too many. We hope, but are not confident, that folks at the national level will get real! Fortunately, curriculum leaders in a number of districts, including ours, have partnered to get clarity around what learners need to know, do, and be like. This knowledge is organized for us into three categories of learner outcomes: content knowledge, reasoning processes, and life-long habits of mind.*

*To begin, we reviewed and studied these three categories of learner outcomes for this <u>age span</u> (not grade level). The district work, which mapped out the progression, pathways, or sequence of the learner outcomes, was very helpful. We identified outcomes our learners have mastered, outcomes they need, and outcomes that might be linked with, or be complementary to, other learner outcomes . . . and through this process, discussion, and debate, we reached consensus as to which learner outcomes to cluster. The clusters were a mix of affective and cognitive outcomes: content outcomes, reasoning outcomes, and habits of mind outcomes.*

*These clusters became the basis for integrated seminars. We were already very adept at creating integrated units of study. So, creating seminars was an easy step for us. We decided the seminars should be no more than 3 weeks or 8-10 class periods. This may change as we become more experienced. Some seminars may be shorter, others longer. We shall see.*

*Our next step was to create cool titles for the seminars. We wanted titles that would catch learner interest and signal that "school" is going to look different. Examples include:*

*Apps for Kids: Making Steve Jobs Proud*
*I'm a Poet and I Know It!*
*A Kid's Life in the U.S.*
*Science IS Everywhere!*
*Around the World in 18 Days*
*Writing for Stephen-King-Wannabees*
*Customs & Cultures: Mine & Yours*
*Point of View: Looking at it Both Ways*

*With seminars we incorporated rather serendipitously something that we discovered was a magical ingredient to learner engagement: CHOICE. We gave them options based on their interests. They had to take some seminars over the course of their three years with us. Others were options. They loved it. When we first started offering seminars, we did it just once — to see how it would go. A few weeks after that initial two-week seminar, I announced to my class that we were going to do another round of seminars. They applauded! Let me say that again. They applauded!!! Seminars are now the rule, not the exception.*

*Let me say a word about how instruction works within the seminar. Please realize this is a work in progress. We come together as Team Five and identify what is working and what needs tweaking. The following are on our "Tweaking" list:*

- ○ *We are now identifying prerequisite knowledge that learners must have mastered to "enroll" in the seminar.*
- ○ *We are identifying online resources for the simpler, foundational outcomes for a specific seminar.*
- ○ *We are wrapping each seminar around a complex reasoning process that we are directly teaching.*
- ○ *We are asking learners for seminars they would like to have created.*

*In summary, here's what's happening: Learners are working on outcomes they need with content that is interesting to them. Learning Facilitators are sharing the load to make this happen. The result: Learners are engaged in learning activities. Learners are meeting with success on the learner outcomes. A win-win for everyone.*

## THE COMBINATION MODEL (Jane's Story)

*I am Jane Spencer, principal of the middle level Learning Community with learners ages 11-13. Brad told you his story of creating the "Workshop Model" for mass customizing learning. Although we are in different buildings, Brad and I meet regularly with Jordan and Michelle. We are on a district level MCL team. We share a commitment to this compelling vision. We have celebrated the successes of each implementation model. And, we have problem solved together the challenges faced in each implementation model. The power of group problem solving is quite amazing! These sessions have brought us to our next goal, which is to combine the Workshop Model and the Seminar Model.*

*Our preliminary plans are to expand the Workshop Model to include an hour in the morning on Math Workshop, an hour on ELA Workshop, and an hour on Complex Thinking Workshop - with Learning Facilitators grouping and regrouping learners as described above and with Learning Facilitators sharing the load. These would focus on the foundational learner outcomes for these areas.*

*The afternoon would be for seminars for application of those morning workshop foundational learner outcomes integrated with more complex learner outcomes in Science, Social Studies, Visual and Performing Arts, etc. This is all a work in progress. We reflect and adjust often.*

*We began this work without technology. We kept track with notebooks and file folders on each learner. Cumbersome, exhausting, but it worked. We created our own spreadsheets and databases to keep and sort data to group and regroup learners. It was primitive, tiptoeing, and perhaps tinkering. But it was a start. We were determined to meet the individual learning needs of our kids.*

*We knew the technology was within reach . . . and so it has come to us. Today's customizing technology has helped us leap into customizing learning. Our ePortfolio system has what I call the "Amazon magic." I am not sure how Amazon customizes for clients. To me, it is magical. Finally, we are seeing that magic in our infrastructure technology. Our ePortfolio, with its magical algorithms, knows the style of the learner, the interest of the learner, and the learning needs of the learner. That data allows us to create Customized Learning Plans for each learner. From that we design the lessons and learning experiences in our workshop and seminar models. And, now we are adding one-to-one devices. MCL is becoming a reality!*

# GUIDELINE # 3: LEARNERS INVESTED IN THEIR LEARNING

The third guideline for the Elementary/Middle School MCL Vision is less tangible. It is about the culture within the classroom. MCL fosters a culture of learning, continuous improvement, and engagement. MCL triggers natural, intrinsic motivation. This is probably the biggest hurdle for some. Many of the "ya' . . . buts" that we encounter are based in old-fashioned understandings of motivation. Many still think students don't like to learn and don't want to learn. And so, we must manipulate them to learn using rewards and punishments.

Designing a learning community in which each learner is learning within his style of learning, at level and pace of learning, with content of high interest IS what creates learner motivation and engagement. "Learners invested in their learning" is the *byprod-uct* of a MCL learning community.

What we do and how we do it characterizes our culture. Key questions to ask OFTEN are:

- *Is what we are doing about learning and support or about control and compliance?*
- *Is what we are doing about learning or doing school?*
- *Is what we are doing about engagement or manipulation?*

The words and actions of learners will answer those questions.

- *Do mistakes fuel their effort / persistence or derail / embarrass them?*
- *Do they embrace or avoid challenges?*
- *Do they welcome or dismiss constructive criticism?*

Listen to their words.

A Little Story *(bmcg)* *If I am asked to work with a Learning Community for multiple days, I ask that everyone read Carol Dweck's book, Mindset. It gives us a common understanding and common vocabulary about, as her subtitle says, the psychology of success. It provides the foundation for understanding that we in schools control the conditions for success . . . and for how a learner views his potential for success. We have the ability to create a culture of "I can get better!" (Growth Mindset); or, a culture of "I either have it or I don't." (Fixed Mindset).*

*With a fixed and growth mindset filter, look at what we say and do in schools. Everything we do is well intended, but in not so subtle ways, we are giving learners messages that they either have it or they don't. How about "Intervention Period?" What's the message? "You go to intervention period, I do not." Instead, let's have a "Power Goal Period" in which everyone has a goal they are working on. Changing one word sends a powerful message.*

*Let me tell a little story here. I may be a bit sketchy on the details of the story, but the punch line said by this 6-year old is accurate.*

> *Three Learning Facilitators, one each in K-2, teamed to group and regroup learners around specific learning goals — not ability / tracking. Learning goals were identified on a progression rather than identified as specific goals for Kindergarten, for Grade 1 or Grade 2. They are just goals for learning. Learners were grouped across age levels depending on the learning goal they needed.*
>
> *One little guy was told he would work down the hall with another Learning Facilitator starting the following day. His home-based Learning Facilitator was a bit worried because he had already been with a number of Learning Facilitators. Now, he was to face a new one. He got off the bus the next day crying. He cried at recess. He cried at lunchtime. Her worry confirmed, his Learning Facilitator asked if he was crying all morning because he was "going to Second Grade?" His response, "What's Second Grade?" She knew once she said "Second Grade" that she was back in the Industrial Age vocabulary of school. Easy to do for even the most avid MCL advocate! And . . . his answer: priceless! By the way, the crying was logical: a forgotten snack, a skinned knee, and spilled milk.*

<u>We</u> create the conditions for success. The problem is the structure. We are reminded of the words of W. Edwards Deming, the Total Quality Management (TQM) guru:

*"Well over 90% of the problem in organizations lies with the structures, not with the people."*

The Industrial Age structures, processes, and procedures prevent us from meeting the individual needs of our learners. Period.

We trust that we have given you enough of the content of *Inevitable* that the remainder of *Inevitable Too! The Total Leader Embraces Mass Customized Learning* will be easy to follow. But we are just paranoid enough to close with a listing of three critical aspects of Mass Customized Learning.

## YOU'RE NOT DOING MCL UNLESS . . .

What differentiates Mass Customized Learning from other change efforts? When will you know that you are indeed customizing learning to each learner every hour of every day? You're not doing MCL unless:

1. ***No Assembly Line Allowed.*** If your system has not replaced the bureaucratic, Industrial Age assembly line, YOU ARE NOT DOING MASS CUSTOMIZED LEARNING. At best you are merely tinkering! That outdated structure is what

causes school systems to be time based rather than learning based. That assembly line structure stops teachers and school systems from applying the most basic and powerful research regarding learners and learning and teachers and teaching.

2. *Total Learner Focus.* If the learner is not at the center of all-important decisions, you are not doing Mass Customized Learning. A total learner focus means:

- We must begin our planning with an understanding of "who is the learner walking through our doors." What has been their experiences, how have they learned to this point, what is their life like outside of school?

- We must ask ourselves what the world will be like that our learners will face when they leave/graduate from our system. What will be their opportunities, what will be their challenges and, therefore, what must they know, be able to do, and "be like," to succeed in that world.

- When we have identified learner outcomes to the best of our knowledge and ability, we then must ask about each outcome, "how is this learner outcome best learned."

- And finally, we must apply today's technologies to restructure our learning communities making it possible to meet the needs of every learner every hour of every day.

3. *Natural Intrinsic Motivators.* If learning is natural, what motivates us to be learners? Today's schools, to a large degree, focus on extrinsic rewards, basically in the form of rewards and punishments. When the rewards and punishments are removed, the behaviors caused by these motivators tend to cease. MCL focuses on four known and powerful intrinsic motivators. Learners are motivated to learn:

a. When the learning is at the optimal level of challenge, not so difficult that it discourages, and not so easy that it's boring,

b. When they are allowed to learn in a learning style that works for them, for some that would be through listening or reading, for others it might be seeing or doing,

c. When the content through which they are learning is interesting to them, and,

d. When they find relevance and meaning in what they are learning.

If you find this description of the MCL Vision to be of high interest and you would like to learn more, we recommend that you read *Inevitable: Mass Customized Learning*.

# REFLECTION: ASSESS AND PLAN

The following self-assessment rubrics (Figures 2.5 – 2.8) might help you to reflect on your knowledge and skills related to *The Mass Customized Learning Vision* and to focus your professional development.

### Reflection Question 1 (Mass Customized Learning)

| **I. SELF ASSESS**<br>(How am I doing?) | *What is the degree to which I understand why Mass Customized Learning is inevitable?* |
|---|---|
| 4  INNOVATING | *I can lead discussions on why and how the Mass Customized Learning Vision is compelling, needed, and doable.* |
| 3  APPLYING | *I can explain how customizing technologies will make and are making it possible to customized learning for learners.* |
| 2  DEVELOPING | *I can explain why and how learners needs (how they think and act) have changed.* |
| 1  BEGINNING | *I can explain why and how the Industrial Age structure is outdated, used to make sense, but doesn't any more.* |

| **II. PLAN FOR IMPROVEMENT**<br>(What do I need to do?) | **III. SUPPORT RESOURCES**<br>(Where can I get help?) |
|---|---|
| *What are strategies that I will do to improve my understanding of why Mass Customized Learning is inevitable?* | *What and / or who are resources that will help me to get better at my understanding of why Mass Customized Learning is inevitable?* |

**Figure 2.5**

**Reflection Question 2 (Mass Customized Learning)**

| I. SELF ASSESS<br>(How am I doing?) | What is the degree to which I understand the Mass Customized Learning Vision? |
|---|---|
| 4 INNOVATING | I can help others understand the Mass Customized Learning Vision. |
| 3 APPLYING | I can explain how Mass Customized Learning is about transformation not tinkering. |
| 2 DEVELOPING | I can define what "Mass Customized Learning" means. |
| 1 BEGINNING | I can explain why having a vision is important. |

| II. PLAN FOR IMPROVEMENT<br>(What do I need to do?) | III. SUPPORT RESOURCES<br>(Where can I get help?) |
|---|---|
| What are strategies that I will do to improve my understanding of the Mass Customized Learning Vision? | What and / or who are resources that will help me to get better at understanding the Mass Customized Learning Vision? |

**Figure 2.6**

**Reflection Question 3 (Mass Customized Learning)**

| I. SELF ASSESS<br>(How am I doing?) | What is the degree to which I understand Mass Customized Learning at the elementary, middle, and secondary levels? |
|---|---|
| 4 INNOVATING | *I can lead others in understanding Mass Customized Learning at the elementary, middle, or secondary levels.* |
| 3 APPLYING | *I have implemented MCL structures and practices at the elementary, middle, or secondary levels.* |
| 2 DEVELOPING | *I can identify starter steps in creating MCL structures and practices at the elementary, middle, or secondary levels.* |
| 1 BEGINNING | *I can create a general picture of what Mass Customized Learning might look like at elementary, middle, or secondary levels.* |

| II. PLAN FOR IMPROVEMENT<br>(What do I need to do?) | III. SUPPORT RESOURCES<br>(Where can I get help?) |
|---|---|
| *What are strategies that I will do to improve my understanding of Mass Customized Learning at the elementary, middle, and secondary levels?* | *What and/or who are resources that will help me improve my understanding of Mass Customized Learning at the elementary, middle, and secondary levels?* |

**Figure 2.7**

**Reflection Question 4 (Mass Customized Learning)**

| I. SELF ASSESS<br>(How am I doing?) | What is the degree to which I understand how Mass Customized Learning is different from other change efforts? |
|---|---|
| 4 INNOVATING | *I can lead others in understanding the "You're Not Doing MCL Unless" requirements.* |
| 3 APPLYING | *I have implemented MCL structures and practices that reflect the "You're Not Doing MCL Unless" requirements.* |
| 2 DEVELOPING | *I can explain the "You're Not Doing MCL Unless" requirements: no assembly line; total learner focus; intrinsic motivators.* |
| 1 BEGINNING | *I am unsure of the difference between Mass Customized Learning and previous or current change efforts.* |

| II. PLAN FOR IMPROVEMENT<br>(What do I need to do?) | III. SUPPORT RESOURCES<br>(Where can I get help?) |
|---|---|
| *What are strategies that I will do to improve my understanding of why Mass Customized Learning is different from other change efforts?* | *What and / or who are resources that will help me improve my understanding of how Mass Customized Learning is different from other change efforts?* |

**Figure 2.8**

# Chapter 3

# The Authentic Leader

*Being Real!*

| ♡ | Profile of<br><br>**THE**<br>**AUTHENTIC EDUCATIONAL LEADER**<br><br>*Leading Consciously and Ethically* |
|---|---|
| MINDSET | Who I am is how I lead my learning community. I must continue my personal development if I am to continue to develop as a leader. I need to be at my best if I am to help this system implement our MCL Vision. |
| PURPOSE | To create a learning community that consistently graduates life-long learners empowered to succeed in a rapidly changing world. |
| CHANGE BELIEF | People will change if there is a compelling reason to change. Our present system isn't working for many learners and is unfair to teachers. MCL holds great promise! |
| PERFORMANCE ROLES | ▶ Creates a compelling mission/purpose for the learning community<br>▶ Models the core values and guiding principles of the learning community<br>▶ Is the lead learner and the lead teacher |
| PERSONAL VALUES | Integrity<br>Honesty |
| PRINCIPLES | Inquiry<br>Contribution |
| THE GURU | Stephen Covey |
| THE EXEMPLARS | Pope Francis, Warren Buffet |
| KEY SOURCES: | • *Leadership: The Journey Inward,* Delorese Ambrose, 2003<br>• *Credibility,* James Kouzes and Barry Posner, revised 2011<br>• *The Speed of Trust,* Stephen M.R. Covey, 2006<br>• *To Sell Is Human,* Daniel Pink, 2013 |

# THE AUTHENTIC LEADER

## *Creates a Compelling Purpose and the Reason for MCL*

We are very serious and we expect that you are too. We want you to know how important you are. Transforming education and schools from the present bureaucratic and stifling Industrial Age assembly line to an Information Age mass customized learning community is critical:

> Critical for learners,
> Critical for our profession,
> Critical for our country, and
> Critical for our society.

That's a heavy load, and our goal is to help you ready yourself for the opportunity and the challenge. But first, some soul searching: *How serious ARE you?*

## HOW BAD DO YOU WANT IT?

Reading *Inevitable* was probably a pleasant and motivating experience for you or you would not have picked up *Inevitable Too!*. The *Inevitable* vision "rang" for you. You knew that it was right, and that it was right for the time. You knew that the MCL Vision was highly "desirable," but if you are like most leaders, you were not so sure about the "doable" boast that we make in *Inevitable*. Effective leaders have a pragmatic side. They are courageous, future-focused, visionaries, but they become realists when they move from the "desirable" question to the "doable" question. Transforming education will NOT be easy. But it can be done and it must be done.

Tinkering with education is easy. Nearly everyone is doing it. Online learning is tinkering, differentiated classrooms is tinkering, flipping the classroom is tinkering . . . good efforts for sure, but none are transformational. We may get small improvements from tinkering, but we will not get the big leap. Any change that perpetuates and supports the assembly line is tinkering. The time-based assembly line delivery of instruction is inconsistent with our most basic research regarding learners and learning; *it has to go!* MCL holds the promise to "leapfrog" today's outdated and tired structures and policies.

Well now, what did reading that last paragraph do for you? Agree? Disagree? Would you take that stand, make those statements, act on those beliefs? Probably with a bit more tact, at the right time and place, but would you share those opinions openly? Would you share them with the board, the staff, parents, learners, the business community? Would you share those beliefs and opinions if it might cost you your job, damage your career, or make you unpopular?

These questions are "how bad do you want it" questions, good for reflection and soul searching prior to pulling the decision trigger. If, after that reflection, you still are as excited about the MCL Vision as you were when you read about Lori Doing Her Learning Plan (Chapter 7 in *Inevitable*) or watched Lori on the YouTube video, then go for it. Expect that you will have good support. We think you will. The rationale for the MCL Vision is logical and strong, but know that there will be those who do not agree and will challenge. We repeat: transforming education will NOT be easy.

*At all times, have the learner in mind, at the center of your decisions.*
*You must be the learner's advocate.*

## THE AUTHENTIC LEADER

The Authentic Leader (AL) Domain is positioned at the center of the TL Framework that we described briefly in Chapter 1. It is placed there because of its importance, and because of its direct and immediate impact on all other domains . . . which is to say that it is at the heart of everything the leader is and does. Do it right, do it consciously, do it ethically, and the other domains will fall into place. Without authenticity, nothing will be easy . . . and success will be in doubt. If you think that this is going to be an important chapter, you're right!

Authentic leaders are not usually very "charismatic." They might be, but they needn't be. Typically, they are ordinary people, much like you and me, who just happen to be doing extraordinary things. Their authenticity comes from their comfort with who they are. Sure, they are growing, working to improve, but they are comfortable in their own skin and they are not trying to fool anyone. They take their relationships and their work very seriously, but they do not take themselves too seriously.

When leadership is genuinely and humbly authentic, we may not even notice its presence. But when leaders lack authenticity, and that lack is exposed either by the routines of the day or by a crisis, trust is lost and everything about leading and managing becomes slow, cumbersome, and problematic. For us, trust is the WD-40 that makes possible a smooth, friction free system able to maximize its resources for the real problems of the day. Personal authenticity creates that trust. Okay, all together now, in unison:

*"Who you are is how you lead!"*

How then might you spot an Authentic Leader? What is she saying or doing? She most likely:

- Is an effective interpersonal communicator. She is a good listener, who paraphrases to ensure understanding, and who openly shares her beliefs, opinions, and feelings. Expect that she will want to know your thoughts about MCL; it will come up in the conversation. She is authentic, AND, directed.
- Has awareness and control of feelings and actions and has a sensitivity and empathy toward others. Daniel Goleman would label this "Emotional Intelligence (E.Q.)."
- Is trustworthy. She will not say one thing to the Board and another thing to the Teacher's Association. She will keep appointments and follow through on commitments . . . that will be her norm and she will expect it of you.
- Is thoughtful and reflective. She will be deliberate when making important decisions (e.g. *We will be a MCL system*) but will act quickly and decisively when necessary. She provides her rationale for important decisions (e.g. *MCL supports our life-long learning goal*) and is willing to change her mind when new data or insights become available.
- Is a team player. Her favorite pronouns are "we" and "our." As in, "We are making good progress toward our vision. Thanks everybody!"
- Is value driven. You will know her values and principles because she talks about them (e.g. *We need to let the fast runners run*) and acts accordingly. She walks her talk, and talks her walk.

In short, Authentic Leaders are those whom many seek out to be their best friend. They have their inner and interpersonal acts together as reflective, open, and honest human beings. But they're more than morally and psychologically healthy people. They lead by example, they are life-long learners and teachers, and they focus the learning community on a compelling organizational purpose: "Empowering All Learners to Succeed in a Rapidly Changing World."

# MORAL FOUNDATION OF THE AUTHENTIC LEADER

We like the "foundation" analogy. Our values and principles are our "foundation." We stand, with both feet on solid ground, when we make decisions and when we act. For the Total Leader, the moral foundation is made up of her personal values, core organizational values, and her Principles of Professionalism. We share our text bookish definitions of each:

- **Personal Values:** Compelling standards of what individuals believe to be right, fair, honorable, important, and worthy of consistent attention and action.
- **Core Organizational Values:** Those values that are widely understood, endorsed, and consistently acted upon by the organization and by each of its members.
- **Principles of Professionalism:** Those ethical rules of decisions and performances that transcend personal considerations and circumstantial pressures to promote the higher good of the organization and its clients.

Authentic Leaders seem to create their moral foundation over time. Their values were partially set by simply knowing right from wrong. We are born with a moral compass. Our parents and teachers and, for many of us, our church helped in our clarification of right and wrong. And we all seem to learn about right and wrong as we experience life. Some things work for us and some don't. By the time we get to a leadership position, we have had ample time and support to know and understand what we value and the principles that will guide our leadership behaviors.

Our favorite Stephen Covey quote, simple and profound, is appropriate here, "If it's important, it should be intentional." We expect that 100% of people in leadership positions would rate "having core values" as very important, yet when we ask groups of leaders if they have put their core values into a written form, our experience is that fewer than 50% say that they have. Covey would say that if your values are important, they should be:

- clear and crisply defined,
- put into writing . . . to add commitment,

- shared with your significant others . . . family and colleagues,
- reflected upon frequently and somewhat systematically, and
- analyzed for their alignment with your decisions and actions.

# VALUES OF THE AUTHENTIC LEADER

We will attach two of the core values that we introduced in Chapter 1 to each of the five Leadership Domains. We have selected those most critical to each domain, knowing that, in real life, we have to act on them all, all of the time. The core values, integrity and honesty, that we define here, are at the center of the moral foundation of the Authentic Leader.

**Integrity:** the long term expression and embodiment of honesty, fairness, trustworthiness, honor, and consistent adherence to high-level principles, especially those recognized and endorsed by one's learning community.

Integrity goes well beyond simply being consistent. We sometimes hear the comment, "He has integrity, he is consistent, if he says that to you, he will say it to everyone."

(cjs) *I have a rancher friend who is "A Ford Man." Now I like the F150 too, but I do go to the Internet and to Consumer Reports before selecting my next vehicle. My friend is a "Ford Man" because his Dad was a "Ford Man." Having integrity is first, knowing your values and beliefs; second, making decisions and taking action consistent with those values and beliefs; and third, stating clearly the value on which you based your decision.*

(bmcg) *As I work with teachers (learning facilitators), principals, and superintendents, I have come to realize that you can't fake it. You can't fake a belief in and commitment to the vision of customizing learning. The vision of MCL has to run through your veins. And...I know it when I see it. I can tell whether or not a person gets and wants this vision. They are not tentative with their words or actions. They speak and act with consistency and conviction no matter their audience because the MCL Vision runs through their veins.*

Let's apply the value of integrity to a learning community. Let's stop for a minute. If we had used the word "schools" instead of "learning community," what would be the picture in our mind? Long hallways? Classrooms on either side? Desks in straight lines? Teachers at the front of a class lecturing, students listening? We would be locked into an Industrial Age mindset. The words we use have power. As we say "learning communities," we envision a MCL school structure. Industrial Age schools are but a faded memory.

Again, let's apply the value of integrity to a *learning community*. How might the AL demonstrate integrity? On what or about what would the leader in this learning community have integrity?

The AL – acting with integrity – would consistently:

1.  Use a new Information Age, mass customized learning vocabulary:
    *schools* become *learning communities,*
    *students* become *learners,*
    *teachers* become *learning facilitators,*
    *courses* become *learning opportunities,*
    *permanent records* become *ePortfolios,* etc.
2.  Never give in to the time-based assembly line delivery of instruction because we know that it is inconsistent with how kids learn, and that it is being applied because it is "administratively convenient" to do so.
3.  Move from the coercive "stick and carrot" extrinsic motivators to the intrinsic motivators of learning level, learning style, personally interesting content, and relevance.
4.  Consciously move the learner to the center of decisions and actions. Always asking questions such as,

    -   Who is the learner walking through our door?

    -   What opportunities and challenges will they face when they leave our learning community?

    -   Is this decision about learning or about control?

    -   And, when we have identified our learner outcome . . . making the next question, "How is this outcome best learned" rather than "how will we teach that?"

We think that the four points made above are critical to the MCL Vision or, for that matter, critical to any system with the intent to transform education. We expect that you will add to this list, that you will be consistent in applying what you truly value, and that you will be seen as an Authentic Leader who demonstrates a great deal of integrity.

If you are to be viewed as having "integrity," you need not only to walk your talk, but also to talk your walk. More about this later, but when people hear what you say, and see what you do, your actions are open to interpretation. If you want people to know why you said that, or why you did that, tell them **why**. Take away the possibility of misinterpretation.

**Honesty:**  being fully transparent, candid, and truthful, while being sensitive to the thoughts, needs, and feelings of others.

Honesty is the prerequisite of integrity, integrity is the prerequisite to trust, trust is the prerequisite to Authentic Leadership, Authentic Leadership is the prerequisite of the Total Leader. Total Leaders walk up that ladder so naturally that it probably doesn't require conscious thought, but missing any of the rungs calls all others into question.

In *The Speed of Trust*, Steven M.R. Covey makes financial genius Warren Buffet his exemplar for authenticity, trust, and success. Buffet, once the richest person in the world, lives in a small, old home in Omaha, drives an old GM car, and can seal billion dollar deals with a handshake (no lawyers need be present), and things begin to happen on Monday. Buffet is authentic, his word is his bond, and his track record of honesty and integrity is a story.

More than simply being open and honest in all interactions, the Authentic Leader is sensitive to conditions. Time, place, and audience can all be critical factors. If at a board meeting you are challenged on a basic premise of MCL, responding clearly, then and there, builds trust and authenticity. To not respond immediately and assertively allows the audience to wonder about your commitment to the MCL Vision. Other sensitive situations may require a specific time, location, and approach.

(cjs) *One of my most difficult tasks as a superintendent was to tell internal candidates that they were not chosen for a leadership position that was open in our system. We had an excellent staff development program and usually had a number of good internal candidates. I didn't like to tell them that they had not been chosen, but knew that I had to, and knew that I had to do it with tact and empathy. Those "difficult conversations" were always face-to-face, usually at the candidate's office or workspace and, when possible, on a Friday afternoon so that they had the weekend to process it all.*

*My preparation for the meeting began with me putting myself empathetically in their shoes, "How would I want to learn this if it were me?" On the morning of the scheduled meeting, on my 20-minute drive to my office, I would rehearse how I would open that meeting, and would run through the questions that I might be asked. I would actually do the conversation out loud, hoping that I wouldn't meet someone on the road who knew me and think me a "case." All of that, and the meeting was still painful for me and painful for my colleague who had not gotten the job. We had a couple of rules in our district that everyone knew and seldom broke. One, "No matter what the conflict, no matter what the message that was being delivered, you MUST treat the person with dignity." Two, "It is always possible to be honest without being brutal." If you need help with that, give me a call and we can role-play the situation using your content . . . my office or yours?*

# PRINCIPLES OF PROFESSIONALISM OF THE AUTHENTIC LEADER

Go back if you would to where this section, *The AL's Moral Foundation* begins and take another look at the definition of Principles of Professionalism. We like what it says. Quite clear, very direct, and very powerful. Not much to argue about there! But where "core organizational values" get a good deal of attention, worthy of a listing in handbooks and on walls, "Principles of Professionalism" get, "What was that again, what did you call them, can you give me an example?" We educational leaders do want to be "principled," and we are, mostly; we want to be "professionals," and we are, mostly. MCL presents a principled, professional vision for education. Our principles are critical to the successful implementation of the MCL Vision. So let's get "intentional" about them.

*(Note:We have created a workshop for leadership teams titled, you guessed it, "Principles of Professionalism." The process involving all members of the leadership team can be completed in about 8 hours. The team exits with a powerful list of principles, and with a practical and concrete listing of behaviors and actions consistent with those principles and those inconsistent with the team's principles. The workshop, complete with slides and facilitator's manual, is available on our website, www.masscustomizedlearning.com.)*

Although all Principles of Professionalism, at times, fit firmly into any one of the five Leadership Domains, we have selected the following two that we think are more aligned with the Authentic Leader Domain.

**Inquiry:** the honest search for personal and organizational purpose, rich and broad perspectives on complex issues, and a deep understanding of ideas and possibilities.

Without "inquiry" as defined here, there would not be a Mass Customized Learning Vision. Although "hiding in plain sight," the popular vision would not have surfaced if there were not a search for ideas and possibilities to solve the complex problems that education faces today. "Inquiring" about the real lives of today's learners, thinking "what if" as Hewlett Packard does, embracing cross-industry learning like Apple, Inc. does, all were part of what allowed the out-of-the-box thinking and the MCL Vision to be born. Principled professionals are inquirers, and they do not limit their inquiries to education.

**Contribution:** freely giving and investing one's attention, talent, and resources to enhance the quality and success of meaningful endeavors.

"Having school," much like we did last year and many years past, might bring forth new problems and tax the school system leader/manager. But transforming a system that has changed little in the last 100 years requires courageous leaders ready to risk their personal and professional wellbeing for what they know is right . . . right for learners and right for our profession. The MCL Vision is the most meaningful of meaningful endeavors to which an educational leader could commit. We like the "freely giving and investing" part of the "contribution" principle.

Those who transform the Industrial Age system into an Information Age customized organization to meet the learning needs of today will be our heroes and heroines. And it won't be one person whose contribution makes it happen. It will have happened because of the contribution (freely given) of all educators. We hope and trust that you want to make your "contribution." (If you think that sounded a bit like your minister asking for your "contribution" when the plate is passed, well yes, for us, saving education has become nearly as important as saving souls.)

## TOTAL LEADER PERFORMANCE ROLES

You may recall from Chapter 1 that each of the five Leadership Domains contains three Performance Roles. (We will be using this label many times throughout the book so allow us to shortcut the label and refer to the Performance Roles simply as "PR" or "PRs.") Our 15 PRs are derived from our study of leadership, change, and futures literature over the past 15 years or so. The PRs are not so much about theory; they are mostly about actions, about what the gurus tell us that effective leaders actually DO. Note the caps here. We are speaking very loudly when we say that the PRs are WHAT EFFECTIVE LEADERS DO.

We believe that the Performance Roles are the most important part of *inevitable Too!*. The purpose of this book is to help leaders apply the Total Leaders Framework to the implementation of the MCL Vision. In a sense, the remainder of this book is not about leadership or MCL. It is about what happens when the two meet. TL is the how; MCL is the what. We expect that you might already know both TL and MCL quite well and that you sense where they are complementary. The Performance Roles sections of the next five chapters of *inevitable Too!* are intended to put the "what" and the "how" together so clearly that leaders have a helpful guide that might make their time and efforts more efficient and effective. Our slogan might be, "We have a strong bias toward the TL Framework and the MCL Vision . . . and we are here to help you." Really, we are!!

Leadership is a complex concept, a complex role, a complex skill, a complex . . . you can take it from here. So know that when we create 15 neat, separate PRs, that we know better than that. On a typical day, and actually in a typical meeting, you will be playing multiple roles simultaneously. Our excuse for the nice neat PR categories is that they are more easily explained if we don't mix too much.

# PERFORMANCE ROLES OF THE AUTHENTIC LEADER

▶ *Creating a Compelling Mission/Purpose for the Learning Community*

▶ *Modeling the Core Values & Principles of the Learning Community*

▶ *Being the Learning Community's Lead Learner and Lead Teacher*

# PR 1: Creating a Compelling Mission/ Purpose for Mass Customized Learning

*In the absence of organizational purpose,*
*leadership does not exist.*

All fifteen of the Performance Roles are important, but *Creating a Compelling Purpose* heads the list. Not only is this Performance Role the most closely associated with the purest definition of leadership, it's also a prerequisite for the other fourteen since an organization's compelling purpose virtually drives everything else it does. But if an organization lacks a compelling purpose, the other fourteen Performance Roles will lack direction and focus and be very difficult or impossible to implement successfully.

Our careers started when principals were hired to "have school." We were sometimes called leaders, but in today's leadership literature we would definitely be called managers. We "did school" the way it was done the year before, maybe with a new textbook series. Our mission was . . . well, to *have school*. Isn't this what we do in late August? If you were good at doing master schedules, disciplining the unruly, supervising the staff, you were a good principal. Textbooks were our curriculum, teacher-centered classrooms the norm, and lectures were the most common form of instructional delivery. The purpose of all of this, the mission of the school system, was assumed . . . and, truth be known, it was to "have school" with the same subjects, the same organizational structure, and the same teaching/learning methods.

In many ways and in many places things have changed. We now seldom find a school system that does not have a mission statement, a set of core values, some form of learner outcomes, and maybe even a vision statement. The problem that we continue to see, however, is that these direction-setting statements are not impacting what happens in the schools or the classrooms. In many cases, the reason for this disconnect is caused by the manner in which the mission and vision were created ("We weren't involved!"), the very content of the direction-setting documents ("What is this supposed to mean?"), and/or the lack of follow-through by the school leader ("And that was the last we heard about it!").

> *The Main Thing*
> *is to MAKE the*
> *Main Thing*
> *the Main Thing!*
>
> **The Power of Alignment,**
> **George Labovitz and Victor Rosansky**

## STRATEGIC DESIGN

(cjs) *Bill Spady, my friend and colleague, and I created a strategic planning process years ago that we believe contains all of the components to make the planning process successful and impactful. What we chose to call Strategic Design has been tested, accepted, and widely considered to be the best approach to strategic planning available to school systems today. We describe it here, not to suggest that this is the only way to set a Strategic Direction, but to help you to know the critical aspects of the planning process that must be considered no matter what the approach or no matter who the facilitator. You may be interested to know that we have used this process with other not-for-profit organizations and businesses . . . and it works for them as well.*

*(Note: We have created a process for training Strategic Design facilitators. The training package includes a comprehensive facilitators guide with accompanying power point slides. Go to our website, www.masscustomizedlearning.com, and look for resources for Inevitable Too! You can also access a sample of a completed Strategic Direction document that was created through the Strategic Design process.)*

Before we begin the discussion of the components of the Strategic Design and the process for its creation, let's be clear about how we expect the Strategic Direction will be used. We want our documents, our contracts if you would, to be read, understood, embraced, and supported by all. Everyone in the system and the community should be informed by our Strategic Direction document. In addition to its communication role however, we fully expect the Strategic Design to be used as a decision screen for every decision, large and small, made for our learning community. It should be "the Bible" for the board, the leadership team, teachers, and staff.

If the Strategic Direction document is to serve these purposes, it should be brief, clear, jargon free, positive, and inspirational. In short, the purpose of the process is to create a compelling direction and a decision screen for everyone, but especially for those who are making important decisions regarding the future of the learning community. It will be the responsibility of the decision makers to make decisions based on the Strategic Direction, and it will be the responsibility of everyone else to hold them accountable for aligning decisions with the Strategic Direction.

## COMPONENTS OF A STRATEGIC DIRECTION

When we introduced the Total Leaders Framework to you in Chapter 1, we shared a listing and a brief definition of the four critical components of a Strategic Direction. This Performance Role, *Creating a Compelling Organizational Mission/Purpose*, provides an opportunity to define each component in more detail by providing examples and a bit of a discussion with each. The Strategic Direction components are linear except for the first two. Do our values drive what our mission is to be, or does our mission drive what our values are to be? The third component, learner outcomes, fits neatly under the mission as outcomes are basically beginning the clarification of what it will take to accomplish our mission. Vision, the fourth component, is a picture of what we will look like, feel like, and be like when we are living our values, accomplishing our mission, and learners are able to demonstrate all learner outcomes.

## *Critical Component # 1:*
## *Values/Beliefs: What we honor and believe ... and therefore, how we do things.*

What we value and believe about learners, learning, and learning communities must ultimately be evident in our vision, a vision that paints a picture of us "doing things." A value or belief is a hollow concept unless we ask the "so what" question. So you believe that "we should be graduating life-long learners," so what? What in our vision will clearly show us that we take that seriously, that our system is designed to consciously and systematically ensure that that happens for all learners?

Our experience has been that we get the best discussions, the best set of beliefs, the best decision screens when we ask:

- What are your strongest beliefs about learners and learning?
- What are your strongest beliefs regarding teachers and teaching?
- What are your strongest beliefs regarding schools and school systems?

Some of the statements that we label as a belief are, in reality, more a fact than a belief. From our point of view, that "learners learn at different rates" is a fact. But no matter what the label, when we design a school or classroom structure, that fact/belief must be given serious consideration. Workshop participants don't care about the label, but they do care about it becoming part of the decision screen. Researchers might say that it is not a fact if it is not supported by rigorous research, but parents and experienced teachers who work with children don't have to go to the research library to substantiate what they "know."

For example, the process for creating the MCL Vision wasn't very linear. We knew the Industrial Age school was outdated and not meeting the needs of learners. We wondered what might replace it. The MCL Vision grew out of *implicit* values and beliefs that we shared. Our shared values and beliefs informed our thinking. We didn't start with articulating our values and beliefs; perhaps we are so in sync that it wasn't necessary. Or, is it that they are so obvious it wasn't necessary! But when we work backwards in the process and ask ourselves today, "What values, beliefs, and research caused us to embrace the MCL Vision?" they would include the following. *Are these your values and beliefs as well?*

## *Values that led us to the MCL Vision:*

We value . . .
- learning, learning for everyone, including us
- learner centeredness when thinking about schools
- equal learning opportunities for everyone, a level playing field
- learners being free, responsible, and productive
- learning success for everyone, to their highest level

*inevitable Too!*

## Beliefs that led us to the MCL Vision:

We believe that . . .
- All children can learn.
- Success breeds more success.
- Learning is natural, we are born learners, learning continues to be natural when the conditions are right.
- Schools control the conditions for learner success.
- Learners are motivated to learn when the learning level is appropriate.
- Learners are motivated to learn when learning in a style that works for them.
- Learners are motivated to learn when the content is of high interest to them.
- Learners are motivated to learn when learner outcomes are relevant to them.
- Technology has opened the door to customizing learning.
- Learners can be trusted.
- Teachers sincerely want to meet the needs of all learners.

## TYPICAL BELIEFS/GUIDING PRINCIPLES

During the Strategic Design workshop with a school system, the group typically creates a list of values/beliefs/guiding principles that become their decision-making screen. Typical statements from a public school's Strategic Design are:

About Students and Learning, we believe that:
- All students can learn, have natural talents, and want success.
- Genuine success and self-esteem are earned through honest achievement.
- Learners progress at different rates, in different ways, for different futures.
- All students need a safe environment where they feel valued.

About Teachers and Teaching, we believe that:
- Teachers build caring relationships that engage students in learning.
- Teachers are innovative, enthusiastic, life-long learners.
- Teachers empower all students to reach their individual potential.

About Learning Communities, we believe that:
- Parents are the student's first teachers.
- Our learning community provides a sense of family.

- Collaborative community partnerships are essential.
- The greatest asset is our people; the highest priority is our students.
- The most successful learning communities are resource rich.

We like to limit the number of bullets to three for each of the categories, but usually we are not successful, and we end with four or five. The problem is that as the list gets longer, each entry becomes less important and less memorable. The Eagle County School District, Vail, CO, where Chuck was Superintendent, had three powerful and unambiguous, easily memorable, belief statements. Everyone knew them, could recite them, and could not duck them. Simplicity is frequently an asset.

- All kids can learn.
- Success breeds success.
- Schools control the conditions for success.

## Critical Component # 2:
## Mission: Why we exist; what business we are in.

Your mission statement is your first and most basic statement of your learning community's purpose. It is the foundation direction setter. It should be brief, ten words or less, memorable, catchy/sticky if it works, descriptive of your purpose for being, tells how your learning community is unique, challenging, and inspirational. It should not be a "slogan" that looks good on your stationery but doesn't state your mission. Your mission statement will drive your learner outcomes, your learner outcomes will drive your curriculum and instruction, and your success with each learner will circle around and show your mission to have been real, to have been accomplished. Sound important? It IS.

One of the first times Bill Spady and Chuck Schwahn facilitated a Strategic Design process, the group created the following mission statement. Word for word, it said,

### *"Empowering all learners to succeed in a rapidly changing world."*

Very powerful and just makes our arbitrary 10-word limit. Other systems have of course created excellent mission statements, and many of them are takeoffs on this original. Improve on it if you can! We will root for you.

This statement is not a slogan. In fact, it won't work for one. But let's take it apart word by word so that we can see its direction setting power . . . and "setting direction" is what a mission's mission is.

### To empower
Not to train, not to educate, not to develop, but to "empower," to put this learner in control of his/her life, not a one shot deal but be empowered to continue learning, to be a life-long learner. Empower, not a slogan, but a powerful statement of personal control and responsibility.

### All
This word doesn't provide any flexibility, no need for bell curves or standard deviations.

### Learners
Not students who require direction, but self-directed learners, learners forever.

### To Succeed
In all walks of life, successful relationships, successful careers, personal happiness.

### In a rapidly changing
Time is past when anyone is finished learning, we must expect that the speed of change will only increase, our grads must be ready for challenges and opportunities the world offers.

### World
Not in your community only, state only, the USA only but the "world." Our grad's world will be global.

So let's put it all back together again and feel the power of the mission:

### *"Empowering all learners to succeed in a rapidly changing world."*

Let's have a little fun here. Some organizations are in a business or industry that lends itself to brief and clever mission statements. We list four mission statements and challenge you to identify the organization or business that it represents. Don't look at the answers until you have given it a good try.

Real Mission Statements

1. Organizing The World's Information
2. 10:30 a.m.
3. Making People Independent Again
4. Producing World-Class Engines and Drive-Trains

Answers: (1) Google, (2) Fed Ex, (3) A Rehab Hospital, (4) Honda,

## *Critical Component # 3:*

## *Learner Exit Outcomes: What we want our graduates to be able to do, to be like, and to know that will directly affect their future success.*

MCL requires learner outcomes, learner accountability, and system accountability. While the MCL Vision is innovative and exciting, it is also logical and systematic, and rigorous. If the learning community's mission is the ultimate purpose of the organization, then learner outcomes must be derived, and ultimately demonstrated by learners if they are to graduate "Empowered to succeed in a rapidly changing world."

This brings us to a very important decision point for the learning community, for its leaders as well as the entire community:

> *Will the learner outcomes be based on* **Life Roles** *(see Figure 3.1)?*
> *Will they be based on the* **Common Core Standards** *developed by educators and supported by state and federal governments?*
> *Or will there be some meshing of the two choices?*

Learner outcomes based on life roles, by their very nature, hold promise to be relevant to learners, while outcomes based on the Common Core Standards tend to be based on our present curriculum, which may help to ensure that graduates will be ready for college. In fairness, the differences between the Common Core Standards and Life Role Outcomes are not as sharp as our comparison might make them appear. The Common Core Standards might include some life-role-type learner outcomes and the Life Role Outcomes can, and will, include learner outcomes that prepare graduates for more school. But which will be the framework that allows the best aspects of the other? Will the framework be Life Roles, or the Common Core?

Our bias is for life-role-based learner outcomes as the basic framework while systematically working in the Common Core Standards as "enabling" learner outcomes.

Without doubt, both the Civil and Global Spheres of Living require that a person must know forms of government. The Economic Sphere requires that they must know Math and Science. The Learning Sphere requires that they must demonstrate reading, learning, speaking, writing skills, etc.

This bias for life-role outcomes is based on what we believe to be one of education's largest problems. Simply and sharply stated, in many schools, our kids are being bored to death. Given the content and the structure of today's schools, who could blame them? Learners do not find our curriculum designed 120 years ago by the Committee of 10 relevant as to content, and they don't relate to the Industrial Age, assembly line, lecture dominated mode of learning.

## AN EXAMPLE: ONE DISTRICT'S STRATEGIC DESIGN

Creating a Strategic Direction for a learning community is so central to everything. The following is an example of one district's work. Our introductory comments are in regular print. The district's comments are italicized. We have named this district the Lincoln Unlimited Learning Center (LULC).

The "Spheres of Living" (Figure 3.1) form the bridge between the learning community's mission and their exit learner outcomes.

## SIGNIFICANT SPHERES OF LIVING

**Figure 3.1**

*The "Spheres of Living" provide the link between our learning community mission, "Empowering All Learners to Succeed in a Rapidly Changing World," and The Exit Learner Outcomes that follow. Our mission implies that LULC graduates will be equipped to live a successful life in the world they will encounter. The question then, for the Strategic Design group, became "where will students live their lives, or, what are the major spheres/arenas of living for successful adults?" Think forward. 1) If we can determine the major Spheres of Living, and then 2) identify the Learner Exit Outcomes for each Sphere of Living, and then 3) graduate young men and women who can demonstrate those Exit Learner Outcomes, the LULC will have **Empowered All Learners To Succeed in a Rapidly Changing World.** The seven Spheres of Living were generated and agreed to by the Learning Community planning group.*

The planning committee of 100+ members was charged with identifying the future conditions graduates would face in each of the seven spheres of living, and then, based on those future conditions, to identify what graduates needed to know, be able to do, and to "be like" in order to live a successful life in that sphere of living.

We share the work of two Spheres of Living groups with you: the Learning Sphere and the Economic Sphere. The first section of each lists the future conditions for that Sphere, followed by the accompanying exit learner outcomes. As you study these learner outcomes, think of what we call the "test of completeness." That is, if the learner can demonstrate each of these outcomes, would they be ready for a successful life in that Sphere of Living.

## FUTURE CONDITIONS of the <u>LEARNING SPHERE</u> of Living

- ▶ We are living in a rapidly changing world.

- ▶ A successful personal and professional life demands life-long learning.

- ▶ Keeping skills up to date, once the responsibility of the company, is now the responsibility of the individual.

- ▶ Much of what we learn becomes obsolete very quickly.

► Technology and the Internet provide powerful tools for finding information and for learning.

► Online learning, customized to the learner, is available on nearly every topic of interest.

► Much of the information in the media and on the Internet is biased and/or inaccurate.

► The amount of new information available is more than anyone is able to consume, comprehend, and/or use.

---

### EXIT LEARNER OUTCOMES
### for the <u>LEARNING SPHERE</u> of Living

*The LULC Graduate is a Self-Directed, Life-long Learner who:*

- Possesses core knowledge upon which to build future learning.
- Reads to understand print material, consumer information, and literature.
- Researches and forms opinions regarding current trends and issues.
- Identifies bias, propaganda, and dishonesty in all forms of media.
- Creates and pursues purposeful and challenging learning goals.
- Acquires, organizes, analyzes, evaluates, and synthesizes information from a wide variety of sources and applies that information to solve problems.
- Takes advantage of learning opportunities created by technologic advances.
- Shares his/her learning with others by teaching and modeling.
- Transfers learning and successful practices to new situations.
- Seeks learning opportunities consistent with future-focused vision of self.

---

## FUTURE CONDITIONS of the <u>ECONOMIC SPHERE</u> of Living

► Customers have high expectations for customized, high quality products and services.

▶ Technology allows a large percentage of business to be transacted from any place at anytime and "doors" are open 24/7.

▶ The world IS flat – the Information Age, the computer, and the Internet allow anyone to compete for work and contracts from anywhere.

▶ Today's high wage jobs go to workers with high level thinking skills, to those who can work with little supervision, and to those who are engaged.

▶ Empowered people are productive and are a competitive requirement in today's economy.

▶ There is little loyalty or job security in today's workplace. Workers must keep their skills sharp and be ready for their next job interview.

▶ Much "knowledge work" can be done from any location, and reliable workers are given a great deal of flexibility in their work location and their hours.

▶ Work teams rather than individuals are usually required to solve today's complex problems.

▶ The economy has gone global and there is a good deal of cultural diversity in today's workplace.

▶ A significant and growing number of people are "free agents" working for themselves rather than for an organization.

▶ Consumers are rewarding businesses and organizations for ethical and moral practices.

▶ Women, in growing numbers, are starting their own businesses and are responsible for much of America's job growth.

▶ Pension plans are a thing of the past; today the responsibility for long-term financial security is with the individual.

---

### EXIT LEARNER OUTCOMES
### for the <u>ECONOMIC SPHERE</u> of Living

*The LULC Graduate is a Quality Producer and Financial Manager who:*

- Knows himself/herself well enough to identify a work life in which he/she will find meaning, purpose, and intrinsic motivation.
- Is a highly motivated, self-directed, flexible, and empowered worker or entrepreneur.
- Is a life-long learner, keeping himself/herself competitive in a rapidly changing world and job market.
- Tracks the trends of the local and global marketplace and the emerging needs of a changing population.
- Identifies quality standards and creates quality products and services in an effective, efficient, and responsible manner.
- Communicates and works effectively in diverse work groups.
- Applies transformational technology to increase quality and productivity.
- Can articulate the basic tenets of capitalism and can apply them to his/her present circumstances and his/her vision for the future.
- Manages and invests financial resources to meet life's needs.
- Can identify a business opportunity and write a business plan that meets loan application standards.
- Considers and acts upon the moral, ethical, and environmental ramifications of business decisions and activities.

---

## Critical Component # 4:
## Vision: Our mental picture of the future we prefer to create.

After reading *Inevitable*, many people contacted us wanting to visit the school that Lori (of Chapter 7 and YouTube fame) attended. We realized then that *Inevitable*, in total, is a detailed description of a vision: the MCL Vision. Visions are most powerful when written in the present rather than future tense, but we didn't realize how "real" we had made Lori's experiences. We now refer to *Inevitable* more often as a vision than as a book. After seeing *Lori Does Her Learning Plan*, everyone seems to want it for their system, for their learners. Tis a tribute to the power of vision.

Leadership is a bit tricky at times. Our early leadership experiences led us to believe that "leadership = influence," but then, when facing the reality of rapid change, we realized that "leadership = future-focused influence." Leaders need to have a sense of future needs and conditions. Did you begin the Strategic Design process knowing that you wanted it to end with a vision for Mass Customized Learning?

We think that you should have! You were hired, or should have been, for your ideas, for your expertise, for your track record of success and, hopefully, for your vision of what a world class learning system could be. You hold a position that allows and requires that you be a visionary. You are the only one who gets that spot. So if you maneuvered the system a bit to get to where you have an opportunity to create a MCL Vision for your system, good for you, you are doing your job, the job you were hired to do. But then, in reality, you have probably been talking about MCL with your board, the leadership team, the staff, and the community for some time, so nothing came as a surprise.

## SUGGESTED VISION COMPONENTS

| | | |
|---|---|---|
| O | Curriculum | *what we teach* |
| O | Learning | *what it is like from the learner's perspective* |
| O | Instruction | *how we teach / learn* |
| O | Assessment | *how we measure learner success* |
| O | Technology | *how we use technology to customize & increase learning* |
| O | Personnel | *our ideal staff* |
| O | Leadership | *at all levels* |
| O | Stakeholders | *our involvement and support* |

**Figure 3.2**

Figure 3.2 lists the components of a comprehensive vision for the entire learning community. It is certainly OK for the group to decide that they want to add or re-label components. It is good to let the group know that you expect to have liberty to add to or modify the work of the vision section of the Strategic Direction. It is not realistic to expect community members to know the "how" part of the plan. Their value is most important in the "what" parts of the plan, the values, the mission, and exit learner outcomes. To give a feel for a vision statement, we share the "Instruction" component from the Strategic Design of a district below.

## Our <u>LEARNING</u> Vision

### *Learning, from a learner's perspective*

- I am very involved in the planning of my learning experiences. My learning coach from school and my parents get involved in helping me set my direction; but as I progress, I am becoming more responsible for my own learning program.
- Every day, I come to school and am met at my developmental learning level, I am challenged, I am usually successful, and I leave school wanting to return tomorrow.
- All LULC students are naturally highly motivated to learn because the learning experiences of each student are matched to their developmental learning level, their learning styles and strengths, and their interests.
- I learn in many ways – about one-half of my learning is online, I take part in numerous seminars with other learners, I attend large group lectures, I read a lot, and I learn from mentors in our community.
- LULC students believe that today's world requires life-long learners, and teachers design learning activities to ensure that graduates leave the school system as self-directed, future-focused, life-long learners. As I advance through my program, I increasingly become accountable for my own learning.
- I have an electronic learner outcome portfolio that shows a complete record of my learning accomplishments. My parents, my learning coach, and my teachers have access to my portfolio.
- Our world is becoming increasingly global and diverse, and LULC learners continuously learn to embrace diversity . . . diversity of cultures, religions, ethnicity, and ways of viewing the world.
- All LULC students leave our school system with the opportunity to choose any future they desire . . . graduates are ready for college, for employment, and/or for creatively designing their own future.
- LULC has become recognized as the place to visit to watch students and adults study, analyze, and debate cultural, religious, economic, and global issues.

As we noted at the beginning of this Authentic Leadership chapter, this first Performance Role is at the center of all 15 PRs. Get it solid or everything else will be a bit off kilter.

# PR 2: Modeling the Learning Community's Core Values and Principles

*"Your whole world is a stage."*

You can't fake authenticity. What you do, what you say are symbols of your core values. *The minute you step out of your car in the morning they are watching you!*

(cjs) *As Superintendent of the Eagle County School District, Vail and Eagle, CO I did five things upon my arrival that were routine for me, but quite significant for others. To me, these were not heroic, nothing out of the ordinary. It's just who I am. While having my usual lunch with the "brown bag" group in the district office coffee room, the conversation turned to my arrival three years earlier. Apparently, I had done five things that surprised and shocked everyone a bit. These things had created a buzz throughout the district. My lunch group said that these five things "told them who I was." I will share these five and in italics what made the rather routine incidents meaningful to the E.C.S.D. staff.*

1. Ten steps inside the district office door, on my first day, I met Mary, the receptionist for the district office. I looked at her nameplate, then looked her in eye and said, "Hey Mary, I'm Chuck and I'm the new superintendent. It's good to meet you. I'm excited to be here."

*No one was expected or allowed to call my predecessor (who was younger than I) by his first name; he was to be "Dr. Smith."*

2. Susan, my secretary who soon became my trusted teammate, showed me to my office. We talked about the district for an hour or so and ended talking about my office setting. Nice view of the Rockies by the way. I asked Susan if maintenance might rearrange my furniture. I wanted the big desk that was in the middle of the office pushed against a wall to be my workstation and wondered if there might be a small round table and four chairs available that I could place by the big window for conversations when people came to the office. I told her I did not want to order a new table and hoped we could find one in a storage room.

*What, no big desk complemented by a big high back chair to intimidate! And a "used" table and chairs! This is Eagle County and Vail for goodness sakes!*

3. At the annual opening of school orientation, my first meeting with the entire ECSD staff, (you've all been there) I was a bit nervous and got a bit warm. After 5 minutes or so on this August day, I casually took off my jacket and tossed it over a chair. A hush fell on the crowd.

*Unbeknownst to me, the new superintendent, there were three rules under which the male administrators (and they were all male) could remove their jackets. You must be in your office, alone, with the door closed. Tossing my jacket over a chair in front of 500 people stole the day; no one remembered the "important" things I said that day but, three years later, everyone remembered "the jacket" incident.*

4. I could not make myself park in the closest space to the office door. There was a sign at the front of that space that read, "Reserved for Superintendent." After a couple of weeks I asked Dick, our maintenance director, to remove the sign when he found time. (Interesting, but after the sign was removed I had no trouble parking in that space when it was open.)

*They thought: You know, this guy just might not put himself above us. Maybe we could be open with him.*

5. I taught the then-new "Madeline Hunter Teaching Skills" course for teachers and principals as part of our staff development program. The structure of the course was designed to demonstrate "Outcome Based Education" (a hot innovative concept of the day).

*They thought: The Supt. risked himself, made a few mistakes, had some good laughs, then went back at it. He appears to see himself as an "Instructional Leader." Maybe we can risk ourselves trying some new ideas, too.*

In short, the message was the culture of the E.C.S.D. was about to change in rather profound ways.

You don't get a choice about "modeling." Everyone is watching, and some are watching when you are "not" there. For better or worse, anyone who chooses to lead is always on stage, not necessarily because they want to be there, but because we put them there. We watch them, we interpret them, and we judge them.

If creating a compelling purpose is the most important thing Authentic Leaders do to generate productive change, then articulating and modeling the organization's core values and Principles of Professionalism are the second most important. Authentic leadership, the central Leadership Domain for the Total Leader, comes down to credibility and trust.

## EIGHT WAYS TO MODEL THE IMPORTANCE OF MCL

How do you "tell" people that MCL is important? Well, for starters, you can say, "Hey gang, I want you to know that the MCL Vision is important to our district and to me; this vision has the power to transform education. I want it badly for our learners, for our learning community. I will need your help to make MCL a reality in our district." And then, you could say it again and again . . . and you should! And some (maybe many) will believe and trust you, and will have confidence that they know where the system is headed and want to be part of it. "Saying" can be a good first step toward communicating the organization's values and beliefs, but in-depth trust comes through acting and through modeling.

The following are eight ways the Modeling Performance Role should be applied to the implementation of *Inevitable: MCL*:

1. **Refer to and use the Learning Community's Strategic Design immediately** and let everyone know that you are doing it. The very next morning is not too soon. Make a significant decision and be clear that that decision is based on the LC's SD. Unused Strategic Designs have the shelf life of a ripe banana if not used immediately and constantly. And once lifeless, they are also as hard to resuscitate as that over ripe banana.

2. **Talk up the MCL Vision.** Everywhere! Everyone! Show your passion for what the vision will do for learners. Know the questions you will get, be ready with logical, fear-reducing responses. Have your 90-second elevator talk ready, your 15-minute Rotary message down pat, and your opening of school 45-minute presentation polished . . . the state leadership association will want you for a keynote. Get the 10-minute YouTube video *Lori Does Her Learning Plan* on your flash drive, show it to the board and at parent meetings. Many districts have made a very strong statement by providing each teacher, principal, and board member with a copy of *Inevitable*. Many have also used *Inevitable* for a "book study." In short, get the MCL buzz going throughout your system and your community.

3. When the buzz is hot, **think of implementing the Strategic Design process** described earlier in this chapter for your system. You will know that you are ready for the Strategic Design process when you are confident that the process will culminate with a personalized MCL Vision for your school district. Just a slight bit of leadership manipulation here.

And YOU need to take the lead here. When we receive a call regarding Strategic Design from a school district, and the call is not from the superintendent, somewhere early in the conversation we will ask . . . in a nice way, "Why isn't the superintendent making this call?" Our experience clearly indicates that if the superintendent/CEO is not invested from the beginning, the process will have little impact. It won't be worth it, for them or for us. Before we end the conversation, we politely state that if there is further interest in the Strategic Design process, we will expect that the next call will come from the superintendent.

4. **Be heavily involved in the Strategic Design work**, from the beginning and all the way through. There is a large "modeling" difference, and consequently a large "impact" difference, between a leader who attends all the sessions and walks around

politely observing what is happening, and a leader who is mixing it up in the small group in which she has expertise and credibility. One models being "above" and the other models "getting feet wet." Our most memorable and most successful SD processes have been when leaders were emotionally involved throughout, who made a bold and coura-geous statement about implementation at the end, and who hit the road selling the SD on Monday morning. Depending on the leader's knowledge and confidence with the MCL Vision and the SD process, we have successfully invited the leaders to be a co-facilitator.

> *"If the leaders don't get heavily and passionately involved,*
> *don't expect anyone else to take it seriously."*

5. **Go on the road.** Depending on the size of your district, **get to every school, early on,** to share a fairly sophisticated draft of the SD with the staff. The purpose of the meet-ing should be to inform, to discuss and answer questions, and to request feedback. Again, depending on the size of your district, it is good to plan ahead and have an administrator and a highly regarded teacher from each school in the district on the planning committee. The three of you should share in the presentation and the discussion. This may seem to be a small factor, but believe us, it is big. Having a principal and teacher supporting the work of the planning committee brings a different and more accepting mindset to the discussion.

Small but impactful points: the draft of the SD should be sophisticated enough to create confidence in its content, but not so polished that it appears to be past the "feedback" stage; having someone official taking notes regarding the feedback from the staff will indicate that the feedback will be seriously considered; talk with the staff about "where from here," about what's going to happen next.

Take your *Inevitable: MCL* "road show" to any service club in the community that will put you on their agenda . . . also, "think" newspaper interviews, TV, your webpage, your blog, social networks, your family reunion . . . well, maybe not the family reunion.

6. **Code your Board Agenda and Leadership Team meetings to your Strategic Design.** When board members receive their packet, each agenda item should be coded to some part of the Strategic Design. (If the item doesn't relate to any-thing in the SD, you might wonder why the item is even on the agenda.) For instance, "this item relates to our curriculum vision, more specifically, it relates directly to the fourth bullet of the curriculum vision. Bonnie, our Director of Curriculum will be with us to answer questions." This coding does two things, one, it helps board members make their decisions should a vote be taken, and two, it lets everyone know that it is our norm to make decisions based on our Strategic Design.

7. **Implement the "Supervision for Alignment" process.** Everyone, at every formal performance review, will discuss the learning community's vision and how their work is helping to make the MCL Vision a reality. The process contains 10 discussion starting questions all of which are designed to align all staff with the learning community's vision. Go to www.masscustomizedlearning.com and look for resources for Inevitable Too!

8. **Always say "we" and "our"** when talking about accomplishments, and "I," "me," or "my" when things don't go quite as you would have liked. Leaders who blame secretaries for problems, even when the secretary may have been at fault, are "modeling" blame and not responsibility.

*You can pretend to care, but you can't pretend to be there.*

Back to the beginning of the Modeling Performance Role, "Your whole world is a stage." We can't remember where we first heard the above quote, but it is reality for a school or school district leader. Your influence with some may be determined by your attendance at a middle school band concert.

# PR 3: Being the Lead Learner and the Lead Teacher

Authentic Leaders lead the quest for continuous personal and organizational learning. For them, learning and being a life-long learner are as natural as breathing. Even if they didn't have an organization to lead, they would be reading a book, listening to someone, trying new things, or simply observing some phenomenon to see what they could learn from the experience.

But lead learners *do* lead organizations and they realize that in our rapidly changing world, continuous learning is required, not just of Authentic Leaders but of everyone in the organization. We agree with Peter Senge that effective organizations, especially those that are effective over time, must be "learning organizations."

Authentic Leaders are open to having new learnings impact them deeply, *even when that learning is less than comforting.* As we look back over the past 15 years or so, we can spot how our learning moved us from acceptance of the time-based, Industrial Age assembly-line school structure, to the Inevitable: MCL Vision. More than simply adding knowledge, meaningful and impactful learning:

* Clarifies or challenges one's values — we have always valued individualized and personalized learning. We always knew that that was the ideal. When we could see and experience how the rest of the world was mass customizing, we knew that we could no

longer accept a system that made time the constant and learning the variable. We began looking for ways to mass customize learning.

* <u>Challenges and maybe changes one's world view/paradigm thinking</u> – why should we continue attempting to compete globally with South Korea and Singapore, who are proving to be better at being obsolete than is the US. Why not apply MCL and "leap-frog" the world educational powers.

* <u>Alters one's expectations</u> – we don't have to accept these dropout rates. If learners are hit at their learning level, if allowed to learn through their best learning modes, if allowed to learn using interesting and relevant content, we can keep them excited about learning and they will stay in school.

* <u>Expands one's vision of the possible</u> – MCL will allow the fast runners to run, fast . . . and far. Look Mom, no ceiling!

* <u>Ultimately changes how one thinks and acts</u> – MCL is obviously inevitable, either we educators do it or someone else will. So let's get on with it. How do we best sell this new vision of education?

And, don't move on here until you've noticed that we've expanded the Lead Learner's role to that of Lead Teacher as well. First, they have to learn and build their understanding, expertise, and fluency with the essential elements of the MCL Vision. Then they have to be able to teach, explain, and defend the MCL Vision to their staff, learners, and community. If they aren't fluent with it, they can't teach it; and if they can't teach it, their Strategic Direction will have a weak knowledge base. It's that basic, and that essential.

The good news here is that Lead Learners/Teachers are intentional about creating learning organizations, and they don't leave anything this important to chance. They model self-directed life-long learning and openly share what they're learning with their people. You'll find them carrying around good books, showing off their new Surface Pro, talking about what they've most recently learned or heard on TED or Gooru, and encouraging others to attend growth-oriented webinars or to check out websites they've enjoyed. Yes, they learn for both enjoyment and purpose, and especially watch for things that relate directly to ways of expanding learning opportunities for learners and improving how their learning community functions.

Moreover, Lead Learners/Teachers encourage, expect, and support continuous learning by everyone in the organization. The question isn't, "Did you read the latest issue of *Educational Leadership?*" it's "What did you think of the *Ed. Leadership* article about the Maine school district that has initiated what they call "Mass Customized Learning?"

Here are some criteria to help you analyze your own Lead Learner attitudes and behaviors. Are you:

O Comfortable with being uncomfortable about what you know and don't know? Lead Learners reflect deeply, and they admit they don't know all the answers.

O A learning addict? Lead learners can't help themselves. They learn even when they have no real need to learn. The true test is that learning doesn't stop with retirement.

O A good listener? Do you ask questions . . . and then really listen, respond, check for clarification, thank the person for sharing, and, if he did, tell him that he just taught you something?

O Hanging out with the bright and the bold, the innovators, the good thinkers?

O Forever young? Can you talk with people much younger than yourself and be in the middle of the conversation . . . and admit your learning "takeaways?"

O Excited about new technology? Do you get the latest? We live in a technological world, and to not embrace technology is to not embrace today's learning.

O The proud owner of a Surface Pro, an iPhone 5 (maybe a 7 before this is published) AND, a wristwatch that gives you the exact yardage from where you are standing to the blue flagged pin tucked away behind the sand trap?

The Learning and Teaching PR should come easy to you. You already have the skills. But knowing that learning and teaching are a big part of your Total Leader role will help you to remember to give those roles focus and attention. Much of your credibility can come from making learning and teaching part of "brand you." Leadership is future-focused influence . . . leadership **requires** learning and teaching.

## REFLECTION: ASSESS AND PLAN

The following self-assessment rubrics (Figures 3.3 – 3.6) might help you to reflect on your knowledge and skills related to *The Authentic MCL Leader* and to focus your professional development.

## Reflection Question 1 (Authentic Leadership)

| **I. SELF ASSESS** (How am I doing?) | *What is the degree to which I understand Authentic Leadership?* |
|---|---|
| 4 INNOVATING | *I can help others understand the role of Authentic Leadership, its function within the Total Leaders Framework, how it is necessary for productive change.* |
| 3 APPLYING | *I seek feedback on and reflect on how I am doing as an Authentic Leader.* |
| 2 DEVELOPING | *I can explain the values, Principles of Professionalism, and Performance Roles of Authentic Leadership.* |
| 1 BEGINNING | *I can identify the characteristics, the mindset, and examples of Authentic Leadership.* |

| **II. PLAN FOR IMPROVEMENT** (What do I need to do?) | **III. SUPPORT RESOURCES** (Where can I get help?) |
|---|---|
| *What are strategies that I will do to improve my understanding of Authentic Leadership?* | *What and/or who are resources that will help me to improve my understanding of Authentic Leadership?* |

**Figure 3.3**

**Reflection Question 2 (Authentic Leadership)**

| I. SELF ASSESS<br>(How am I doing?) | What is the degree to which I have created and work from a compelling purpose for our Learning Community? |
|---|---|
| 4  INNOVATING | *I can help others understand the importance of having a Strategic Direction and how it is used.* |
| 3  APPLYING | *I use our Learning Community's Strategic Direction as a decision-making screen for all work of the organization.* |
| 2  DEVELOPING | *I have led stakeholders in our Learning Community in deriving a compelling purpose resulting in our Strategic Direction (mission, beliefs/guiding principles, exit outcomes, and vision).* |
| 1  BEGINNING | *I can define the components of a compelling purpose for a Learning Community: mission, beliefs/guiding principles, exit outcomes, and vision.* |

| II. PLAN FOR IMPROVEMENT<br>(What do I need to do?) | III. SUPPORT RESOURCES<br>(Where can I get help?) |
|---|---|
| *What are strategies that I will do to create and work from a compelling purpose (Strategic Direction) for our Learning Community?* | *What and/or who are resources that will help me to create and work from a compelling purpose (Strategic Direction) for our Learning Community?* |

**Figure 3.4**

## Reflection Question 3 (Authentic Leadership)

| I. SELF ASSESS <br> (How am I doing?) | What is the degree to which I model the Values, Beliefs, and Guiding Principles of Mass Customized Learning? |
|---|---|
| 4 INNOVATING | *I can help others understand the importance of having and modeling Values and Beliefs/Guiding Principles of the MCL Learning Community.* |
| 3 APPLYING | *I explain to others which MCL Values and Beliefs/Guiding Principles I am modeling, and how and why I am doing so. (Talk the walk)* |
| 2 DEVELOPING | *I model the Values and Beliefs/Guiding Principles of our MCL Learning Community. They "run through my veins." (Walk the talk)* |
| 1 BEGINNING | *I do not work from a set of explicitly stated Values and Beliefs/Guiding Principles.* |

| II. PLAN FOR IMPROVEMENT <br> (What do I need to do?) | III. SUPPORT RESOURCES <br> (Where can I get help?) |
|---|---|
| *What are strategies that I will do to improve my modeling of the Values and Beliefs/Guiding Principles of our Learning Community?* | *What and/or who are resources that will help me improve my modeling of the Values and Beliefs/Guiding Principles of our Learning Community?* |

**Figure 3.5**

**Reflection Question 4 (Authentic Leadership)**

| I. SELF ASSESS<br>(How am I doing?) | What is the degree to which I am<br>the lead learner and lead teacher? |
|---|---|
| 4  INNOVATING | *I encourage, expect, and support continuous personal and organizational learning.* |
| 3  APPLYING | *I can teach and explain the Mass Customized Learning Vision to staff, to learners, to community members.* |
| 2  DEVELOPING | *I can identify defining moments in my learning that shifted my thinking from accepting the time-based, Industrial Age assembly-line school structure to the MCL Vision.* |
| 1  BEGINNING | *I am comfortable with being uncomfortable about what I know and don't know.* |

| II. PLAN FOR IMPROVEMENT<br>(What do I need to do?) | III. SUPPORT RESOURCES<br>(Where can I get help?) |
|---|---|
| *What are strategies that I will do to improve my being the lead learner and lead teacher in my Learning Community or Learning Center?* | *What and/or who are resources that will help me improve my being the lead learner and lead teacher in my Learning Community or Learning Center?* |

**Figure 3.6**

Chapter 4

# The Visionary Leader

*Looking Beyond!*

| | Profile of<br><br>**THE**<br>**VISIONARY EDUCATIONAL LEADER**<br>*Leading Creatively with Cutting-Edge Perspectives* |
|---|---|
| MINDSET | Leaders must be future-focused visionaries, and the MCL Vision has great potential for our learning community. I must start "talking it up" with all role groups. This IS big! |
| PURPOSE | To create a bold, inspirational, and concrete picture of what our learning community will look like, feel like, and be like when we have implemented the MCL Vision. |
| CHANGE BELIEF | People will want to change when they can see a concrete picture of the inspirational MCL Vision, and, when they know how they personally fit into and contribute to making that picture a reality. |
| PERFORMANCE ROLES | ▶ Defines a preferred learning community future<br>▶ Consistently employs a "learner and learning" focus<br>▶ Expands learner, staff, and learning community options |
| PERSONAL VALUES | Openness<br>Courage |
| PRINCIPLES | Future Focusing<br>Clarity |
| THE GURU | Tom Peters |
| THE EXEMPLARS | Jeff Bezos, Amazon CEO; Meg Whitman, Hewlett-Packard CEO, also former CEO of eBay |
| KEY SOURCES: | • *Getting Smart: How Digital Learning Is Changing the World,* Tom Vander Ark, 2012<br>• *The OneWorld School House,* Salman Khan, 2012<br>• *Seeing What's Next,* Clayton Christensen, Scott Anthony, and Erik Roth, 2004<br>• *One Size Does Not Fit All,* Nikhil Goyal, 2012<br>• *Inevitable: Mass Customized Learning,* Charles Schwahn and Bea McGarvey, 2012 |

# THE VISIONARY LEADER

## Creates a Concrete Picture of the MCL Vision

*"If your vision sounds like motherhood and apple pie,
And is somewhat embarrassing, you are on the right track."*

### Peter Block

Today, leadership, visioning, and change feel and sound like synonyms. "You can't have one without the other." Could we add a melody to that quote, you might remember the song. When leadership equaled management, when vision quests were something Native Americans did, and when change was what the new Ford looked like, being a visionary wasn't nearly so critical. Today it is a requirement in every business, profession, or industry. Jack Welch, famous past CEO of General Electric, warned us 15 years ago that, "If your organization wasn't changing at least as fast as the world around it, you were on your way out." Educators seem to have missed that message . . . that was, until the arrival of the Mass Customized Learning Vision.

## THE VISIONARY LEADER

Authentic Leaders are charged with clearly identifying the mission and purpose of the learning community, while Visionary Leaders are charged with creating a concrete picture of what the learning community will look like, feel like, and be like when operating at its ideal best to accomplish its purpose: *Empowering All Learners to Succeed in a Rapidly Changing World.* We learned in the last chapter that people do not change unless they *see a REASON to change.* Here we learn that people do not change unless they can see a *concrete PICTURE of the change* – and that's what Visionary Leaders are there to create. Organizational vision is the concrete picture and a manifestation of the organization successfully pursuing its purpose/mission. It's what the organization will look like when it consistently and creatively acts on its moral foundation and meets its compelling purpose/mission.

The essence of Visionary Leaders is paradigm-breaking imagination and innovation. For them, dreaming, creating, visioning, and innovating is the fun part of being a Total Leader. They excel at creating novel possibilities that others don't see, and charting new directions and destinations for their organizations. They thrive on translating shifts and trends into productive options that transform their learning community. They look for creative options before declaring a preferred course of action, and they never mindlessly opt for the way things have always been done before. Vision is what brings excitement to the productive change process.

*Visions don't push people.*
*They pull people.*

## MORAL FOUNDATION OF THE VISIONARY LEADER

Like all effective leaders, Visionary Leaders operate from a clear moral foundation. The most relevant foundations for the VL are the core values of openness and courage and the Principles of Professionalism of future focusing and clarity.

## VALUES OF THE VISIONARY LEADER

**Openness**: is grounded in a sense of psychological security. It reflects a willingness and desire to receive, consider, and act ethically on information, possibilities, and perspectives of all kinds.

What does the future hold for education; what are our options; what will serve our learning community the best? This isn't a time for acting on bias or ego. It's a time for facing reality and acting in the best interest of the learner, the staff, and the learning community.

**Courage**: the willingness of individuals and organizations to risk themselves despite the likelihood or perception of negative consequences, or fear of the unknown.

The question can't be, "What will I do?" The question is, "What's the right, and courageous thing to do?" Boldly laying one's self, reputation, and future all on the line is the Visionary Leader's way. Their motto: "Win some, make some mistakes, learn a lot!"

# PRINCIPLES OF PROFESSIONALISM OF THE VISIONARY LEADER

**Future Focusing**: conducting a thorough and consistent study of the shifts, trends, and future conditions that redefine a profession, industry, or organization, and taking a visionary and far-reaching view of emerging possibilities.

Put quite simply, leadership is future-focused influence. Leading is a future-focused event. In a world of constant change, Visionary Leaders need to see around corners and over the horizon. Their "sticky phrase" is "Looking Beyond!"

**Clarity**: embodied in the open, honest, and articulate communication of one's direction and priorities, the information needed for making sound decisions and taking positive action, and the expectations that surround work and personal relationships.

Fuzzy and/or differing expectations may be the #1 cause of conflict between people in learning communities. Visionary Leaders honestly and openly articulate their motivations, directions, priorities, and expectations. No surprises!

# PERFORMANCE ROLES OF THE VISIONARY LEADER

Visionary Leaders share with Authentic Leaders the challenge of creating urgency for change and the promise of change in their organizations. They do it by applying their three critical Performance Roles directly to this direction-setting process. The VL's three Performance Roles are:

> ▶ *Defining and describing a MCL future for their learning community*
>
> ▶ *Consistently employing a learner focus*
>
> ▶ *Expanding options for their learning community*

# PR 4: Defining and Describing an Ideal Mass Customized Learning Future for Their Learning Community

*"Powerful visions run well ahead of our present capacity to do them."*

Leaders take people to places they wouldn't go without them. Visions take our breath away. When President Kennedy said in the early 60s that *by the end of the decade the U.S. would put a man on the moon*, he was describing a vision. At the time, NASA knew about 15% of what they needed to know to pull off that vision. No one at NASA said, "Well, until he's listed the details of how to do that, I'm not buying in." MCL is education's "man-on-the-moon" vision.

Consider the words of Gary Burnison in his book, *The Twelve Absolutes of Leadership*:

*"As a leader, you paint the outline,*
*allowing others to collaboratively fill in the canvas."*

President Kennedy painted the outline, NASA filled in the canvas. Similarly, in our book, *Inevitable*, we "painted" the outline for the now possible customized learning. And, as you will see, teams of learning facilitators (teachers), when empowered, are filling in the canvas. Powerful to see!

Creative and bold visions are simultaneously exciting and scary. We don't think that most visions arrive in the minds of visionaries as concrete and well defined. For us, the MCL Vision began more as a dream or a fantasy. We are reminded of Joel Barker's suggestion that we ask ourselves, "What is it, that is impossible to do in our organization today, but if we could do it, it would transform our profession?" Our answer to Joel was, "What if we could meet the personal learning needs of each learner every hour of every day?" That would have been a fantasy before digital technology burst onto the scene. But not any more. It's doable. Desirable for a long time, but doable today.

The "scary" part of creative and bold visions begins to disappear if and when the visionary begins to paint a concrete and comprehensive picture of the vision. MCL is the rather scary label for the vision, but *Inevitable: Mass Customized Learning* is the concrete picture that begins to diminish the "scare" and promotes the "hope." We believe that, today, the "hope" of MCL is stronger than the "scare," and that is the reason for the popularity of the vision, the reason educators are embracing MCL, and the reason professionals are working to make the vision a reality. Visionaries must have a pragmatic side if the vision is to be desired, tried, and successful.

*Visionary Leaders paint a concrete picture of the change,*
*and help everyone to know how the change will impact them personally.*

# VISIONS AT EVERY LEVEL, IN EVERY DEPARTMENT

Up to here, we may have created the expectation that the leader of the system must be THE visionary. In many, probably most cases, the leader does take the central role in the creation and communication of the organizational vision, but that does not have to be the case. Visionaries are throughout the learning community. Visionary Leaders listen to them when they start a sentence with, "What if we . . ."

Visions gain support when they are perceived as created by teams, even when one person had the first big hit on a great idea and others helped to fill in some blanks. When it comes to visioning, it is prudent for leaders to say "we" and "us" and to make those pronouns more authentic when they tell of the specific contributions of others, for example: "The primary team at West Elementary showed us how complementary team teaching, non-grading, and multi-age grouping could be. That was a BIG advance for us."

We expect that the MCL Vision will be seen as the learning community's vision, and that leaders will want this for all learners, for all teachers, and in all learning centers (schools). But the vision won't be, and shouldn't be the same for all. MCL requires that learner needs always be at the center of decision-making. Yet, the needs of middle level learners are different from those of elementary learners, the needs of learners in one community may be different from others, etc. So how do we deal with that?

Within the bounds of the system's MCL Vision, each learning center and each department should create its own vision, a vision that fits the needs of that operation. Each secondary learning center should create a vision statement that meets its unique needs while remaining true to the vision of the central learning community, each middle level learning center a vision, each elementary learning center a vision.

Using the definition for vision, "what will we feel like, look like, and be like when we are operating at our ideal best," what does the MCL Vision mean for curriculum and instruction, for human resources, the business office, the transportation department, food service, etc.? These departments are critical to the effective operation of a learning center and learning community, and their operations will have to change to accommodate the new learner vision. Departments must remember that:

a)    They are key to the implementation of the vision,
b)    They exist to serve the learner and the system, and
c)    Every department is in the "learner learning" business.

Briefly stated, the vision for specific departments might be:

## Curriculum and Instruction:

All curricula is written as measureable learner outcomes and based on Life Roles and/ or the Common Core. All instruction is aligned with "how is the learner outcome best learned" question.

## Technology:

Infrastructure technology or software that makes "Lori Does Her Learning Plan" a reality is created or purchased. All outcomes best learned online are available to learners 24/7.

## Human Resources:

Staff selection tools consciously and systematically look for people who believe in the MCL Vision. Reward systems encourage the implementation of MCL.

## Business Office:

The budget system, format, and vocabulary mirror required MCL expenditures. Government or private grants that encourage MCL-focused innovative approaches to educational reform are sought and received.

## Transportation:

The transportation system meets the flexible transportation requirements of the MCL Vision. The transportation system – to some degree – functions like today's public transportation.

## Food Service:

The menus and food service system are flexible which is required when each learner has his/her one-of-a-kind schedule.

We trust that at this point we have made the case for the Visionary Leader and for Visionary Leaders everywhere. We live in a rapidly changing world. To be and remain successful, we must watch the horizon for what's coming, and we must change to accommodate new realities. We educators have been behind the curve when it comes to meaningful, transformational change. The MCL Vision has the potential to "leapfrog" today's attempts to "modify" our outdated Industrial Age structure.

There will be challenges and setbacks; we will learn from them. We need to be creative and bold! We need to go for it! We need to plan well of course, to minimize risk, but we can no longer sit on our hands. That would not be leadership. That would not be fair to learners, to our profession, to our society. AND, we need to **feel a sense of urgency** regarding MCL.

# YOUR VISIONARY "TO DO" LIST:

We leave you with your Visionary Leader "to do" list. Be ready! As a Visionary Leader:

### You Are the Seeker of the Vision:
- Study the future;
- Watch how other professions and businesses are meeting the needs of their clients, and apply those strategies to creating visions to meet the needs of learners;
- Embrace the MCL Vision.

### You Build Consensus Around the Vision
- Involve people in the change process at every opportunity;
- "Sell" the potential of the MCL Vision;
- Say "we" rather than "I."

### You Communicate the Vision
- Understand the "big picture" aspects of MCL;
- Think through the implications the vision has for everyone, for all role groups, for all positions;
- Understand MCL and communicate it confidently.

### You Clarify the Vision
- Be prepared for the inevitable "what do we do now" questions;
- Extrapolate from new realities and respond with suggestions consistent with the essential elements of the MCL Vision.

### You Model the Vision
- Walk your talk and talk your walk – at every opportunity explain how the things you/we are doing relate to the MCL Vision;
- Build trust through honesty, integrity, competence, and accomplishment;
- Let them know you personally and what your life is about.

### You Are the Keeper of the Vision
- Understand your responsibility to "Keep the Main Thing, the Main Thing;"
- Show your belief in what the MCL Vision can do for learners and that you are in it for the long haul.

# PR 5: Consistently Employing a Learner Focus

There has been a profound switch of power in the past 10 years or so. "The Customer IS King." Every business, still in business, knows that power flip well. Customers ~~expect~~ demand that products and services be customized to meet their needs, that those products and services not cost more than the one-size-fits-all of the past, and they want you to do it with eye contact, a smile, and a soft chair and coffee if they have to wait. When customers evaluate you, and talk with their friends, it's not just about the product or the service; it's about the "total experience." As the business owner, you read customer evaluations when you Google your product/service evaluation. So do potential customers, prior to the time they make their decision to buy from you.

"How," you ask, "does this relate to schools, to teachers, to school administrators, to the curriculum, to instruction? We are not in business, schools are not a business." We could argue about that, but surely we would agree that the learner is our customer. He/she is why our learning communities exist and we should be honoring that position and status; we should be meeting their learning needs; we should be concerned about their "total experience."

Please don't take this to mean that learners make all the decisions. We are the adults, we set the boundaries, we set the expectations and the standards. We must be in control. But much like businesses retaining customers through quality service, we have the opportunity to create motivated learners who love school through high quality customized learning opportunities.

We believe being "learner focused" means paying attention to and operating from the following learner related constructs:

## Who are our learners? How do they think and act?

For starters, we should be learner focused even before the children and young adults walk through our school doors.

Technology has significantly changed how we learn. Anyone can learn just about anything from anywhere 24/7. This 24/7 accessibility shifted the power of learning to the learner. That powerful shift ushered in "The Age of Empowerment" for young and old. Technology made learning interactive and exciting and made lectures seem boring. Technology allows learners to choose the "whats," the "whys," and the "hows" of learning. Being learner focused requires that we take these "outside of school learning realities" into account when designing the learning community. MCL does that. Expect learners to be more highly, more intrinsically motivated as a result. We are seeing it in classrooms already.

## What are learner outcomes?  How do we prepare learners for 21st Century life?

Why do we want learners to learn what we are teaching?  How is what we teach, and expect students to learn, relevant to today's world, to today's learner?  How thoughtful are we educators about these questions?  We believe that much of today's courses and curriculum are there because they have been handed down to us.  Much of it is probably right and good, but we don't believe there is a solid rationale for today's courses or curriculum.  It's there because it's always been there.  Learners learn it because they are told to learn it and because they will need it when they get to the next grade or next school.  Not a highly motivating rationale for learners!

In Chapter 3 we suggested learner outcomes and a curriculum designed down from a learner-centered mission and the seven Spheres of Living be part of your Strategic Design.  Relevance, meaning, and motivation are built in from the beginning.

How about sending graduates out the door who are:

- ○ Self-actualizing individuals (Personal Sphere of Living)
- ○ Self-directed, life-long learners (Learning Sphere of Living)
- ○ Empowering friends (Relationship Sphere of Living)
- ○ Involved citizens (Civic Sphere of Living)
- ○ Caring stewards (Global Sphere of Living)
- ○ Quality producers (Economic Sphere of Living)
- ○ Enlightened contributors (Cultural Sphere of Living)

All seven labels followed by learner outcomes that would have to be "demonstrated" prior to graduation.  Well-written learner outcomes describe what the learner must do to demonstrate learning.  Those demonstrations become part of her ePortfolio.

## How do we engage our learners?  What motivates them?

This topic is covered in some detail in the "You're Not Doing MCL Unless" section in Chapter 2.  As a reminder, we will paraphrase here:

Learners are motivated to learn:

a)   when the learning is at the optimal level of challenge, not so difficult that it discourages, and not so easy that it's boring,

b) when learners are allowed to learn in a learning style that works for them; for some that would be through listening or reading, for others it might be seeing or doing,

c) when the content through which learners are learning is interesting to them, and

d) when learners find relevance and meaning in what they are learning.

# PR 6: Expanding Their Learning Community's Options

If creating an exciting vision that propels the organization forward is the essence of the Visionary Leadership Domain, then "Expanding Their Learning Community's Options" gives everyone in the learning community permission to think as a visionary, to consider and formulate options that are truly outside-the-box (OTB), and to expand organizational perspectives and choices. Visionary Leaders clearly let everyone know that they have permission to think OTB, that they are expected to think OTB, that they will be rewarded for thinking OTB, that people will be listened to when they start their sentence with "What if we . . ."

Whether creating a MCL Learning Community, or going beyond MCL to design complementary visions of your own requires that you grasp the critical elements of MCL:

- ○ No assembly line allowed,
- ○ Meet everyone at their learning level,
- ○ Think intrinsic motivators,
- ○ Ask "how is this best learned" for each learner outcome

. . . and you are ready to fly!

The following is a final reminder of the importance of vision.

---

*Your Vision Is:*

- • Your IDEAL
- • Your ASPIRATION
- • Your TARGET
- • Your BLUEPRINT
- • Your CRITERION
- • Your STANDARDS

*In short, it's your TOTAL FOCUS*

---

# REFLECTION: ASSESS AND PLAN

The following self-assessment rubrics (Figures 4.1 – 4.4) might help you to reflect on your knowledge and skills related to *The Visionary MCL Leader* and to focus your professional development.

**Reflection Question 1 (Visionary Leadership)**

| I. SELF ASSESS (How am I doing?) | What is the degree to which I understand Visionary Leadership? |
|---|---|
| 4  INNOVATING | *I can help others understand the role of Visionary Leadership, its function within the Total Leaders Framework, how it is necessary for productive change.* |
| 3  APPLYING | *I seek feedback on and reflect on how I am doing as a Visionary Leader.* |
| 2  DEVELOPING | *I can explain the values, Principles of Professionalism, and Performance Roles of Visionary Leadership.* |
| 1  BEGINNING | *I can identify the characteristics, the mindset, and examples of Visionary Leadership.* |

| II. PLAN FOR IMPROVEMENT (What do I need to do?) | III. SUPPORT RESOURCES (Where can I get help?) |
|---|---|
| *What are strategies that I will do to improve my understanding of Visionary Leadership?* | *What and/or who are resources that will help me to improve my understanding of Visionary Leadership?* |

**Figure 4.1**

**Reflection Question 2 (Visionary Leadership)**

| I. SELF ASSESS (How am I doing?) | What is the degree to which I define and describe the ideal Mass Customized Learning future for the Learning Community? |
|---|---|
| 4  INNOVATING | *I ensure that all work in the Learning Community is moving toward the MCL Vision. (Keeper of the vision)* |
| 3  APPLYING | *I can respond to "what do we do now" questions with suggestions consistent with the MCL Vision. (Clarifier of the vision)* |
| 2  DEVELOPING | *I "paint the outline" of MCL, and "allow others to collaboratively fill the canvas." (Communicator of the vision)* |
| 1  BEGINNING | *I expect that each department or Learning Center creates its own vision of what they will look like when they have realized the MCL Vision. (Consensus builder around the vision)* |

| II. PLAN FOR IMPROVEMENT (What do I need to do?) | III. SUPPORT RESOURCES (Where can I get help?) |
|---|---|
| *What are strategies that I will do to define and describe the ideal MCL future for our Learning Community?* | *What and/or who are resources that will help me to define and describe the ideal MCL future for our Learning Community?* |

**Figure 4.2**

**Reflection Question 3 (Visionary Leadership)**

| **I. SELF ASSESS** (How am I doing?) | What is the degree to which I am consistently learner focused? |
|---|---|
| 4  INNOVATING | *I expect and ensure that learners become empowered decision makers in the creation of their customized learning plans.* |
| 3  APPLYING | *I expect and ensure that outcomes for learners are based on 21$^{st}$ Century Life Role Outcomes.* |
| 2  DEVELOPING | *I expect and ensure that all work is based on our digital native learners: how they think and act and what engages them.* |
| 1  BEGINNING | *I expect and ensure all decisions are screened through the "is this about control or learning" question.* |

| **II. PLAN FOR IMPROVEMENT** (What do I need to do?) | **III. SUPPORT RESOURCES** (Where can I get help?) |
|---|---|
| *What are strategies that I will do to improve my consistent and uncompromising focus on learners?* | *What and/or who are resources that will help me improve my consistent and uncompromising focus on learners?* |

**Figure 4.3**

**Reflection Question 4 (Visionary Leadership)**

| **I. SELF ASSESS**<br>(How am I doing?) | *What is the degree to which I expand options for the Learning Community?* |
|---|---|
| 4  INNOVATING | *I seek out innovative partners and thinkers to help shape and communicate our MCL Vision.* |
| 3  APPLYING | *I implement structures and practices that propel our Learning Community toward our MCL Vision.* |
| 2  DEVELOPING | *I expect and encourage out-of-the-box thinking / ways to realize our MCL Vision. I study future conditions and technology that can aid in customizing learning.* |
| 1  BEGINNING | *I am an out-of-the-box (OTB) thinker resisting the pull of the Industrial Age, assembly-line structure of schools.* |

| **II. PLAN FOR IMPROVEMENT**<br>(What do I need to do?) | **III. SUPPORT RESOURCES**<br>(Where can I get help?) |
|---|---|
| *What are strategies that I will do to expand options for our Learning Community?* | *What and / or who are resources that will help me expand options for our Learning Community?* |

**Figure 4.4**

## Chapter 5

# The Relational Leader

*Reaching Out!*

| | Profile of<br><br>**THE**<br>**RELATIONAL EDUCATIONAL LEADER**<br><br>*Leading Collaboratively and Collegially* |
|---|---|
| MINDSET | We are into the MCL Vision as a team. Everyone has something to offer. We share everything – both the blame and the glory. I need to be a good listener! |
| PURPOSE | To create a learning community culture of collegiality, cooperation, innovation, quality, and success. |
| CHANGE BELIEF | Change happens from the inside out. When individuals and teams are involved, have ownership, and are committed to the MCL Vision, change will happen. |
| PERFORMANCE ROLES | ▶ Develops an open, change-friendly MCL culture<br>▶ Involves everyone in the MCL change process<br>▶ Creates meaning for everyone |
| PERSONAL VALUES | Integrity<br>Commitment |
| PRINCIPLES | Inclusiveness<br>Win-Win |
| THE GURUS | Daniel Goleman and Dr. Phil |
| THE EXEMPLAR | Oprah Winfrey |
| KEY SOURCES: | • *Primal Leadership: Realizing the Power of Emotional Intelligence,* Daniel Goleman, 2002<br>• *Integrity,* Stephen Carter, 1996<br>• *The Seven Habit of Highly Effective People,* Stephen R. Covey, 1989<br>• *Organizational Culture & Leadership,* Edgar H. Schein, 2010 |

# THE RELATIONAL LEADER

## Creates the Commitment to the MCL Vision

*"Seek first to understand, then to be understood."*

### Stephen R. Covey

Relationships are where it's at! We always knew the critical nature of relationships when it came to marriage, family, children, grandchildren, friends, and golfing partners, but in the Age of Empowerment, the importance of relationships has taken a center spot, in the Total Leaders Framework. This domain doesn't replace the Authentic Leadership Domain as the "heart," but it, as well as the remaining three domains, completes and powers the TL Framework. We are successful in school and at the university because of our intelligence, we get our first job because of our academic record, but from there on out, we make it because of our ability to establish and maintain healthy relationships . . . or get fired because "we can't get along with people."

Relational Leadership may seem a warm, soft, and fuzzy domain. But don't let it fool you; it is important, powerful, even critical. Without willing involvement of stakeholders, the motivational energy and impetus necessary for making both Strategic Direction Setting and Strategic Alignment happen just won't be there. Great ideas and possibilities are one thing; motivation and persistence are another.

Daniel Goleman is our favorite Relational Leadership guru and first on our resource list at the beginning of this chapter. In *Primal Leadership: Realizing the Power of Emotional Intelligence*, Goleman provides us with a framework for the "management of self and relationships" which is the bedrock of Relational Leader success. Goleman's "Emotional Intelligence Domains" are: Personal Competence (*how we manage ourselves*); and Social Competence (*how we manage relationships*). Relational Leaders are aware of

107

their own emotions, and thus are better able to control them. This is key to their ability to sense the emotions of others and build healthy and lasting relationships with them. Goleman's work is an excellent resource and foundation for Relational Leaders seeking to refine or develop their intrapersonal and interpersonal skills.

## MORAL FOUNDATION OF THE RELATIONAL LEADER

You have seen the value of integrity before in the Authentic Leader Domain, but we must also attach it to the Relational Leader Domain. It is a key value throughout, but certainly critical for the Authentic and Relational Leader. Commitment, inclusiveness, and win-win are perfect and natural fits for the RL.

## VALUES OF THE RELATIONAL LEADER

- **Integrity:**    the long-term expression and embodiment of honesty, fairness, trustworthiness, honor, and consistent adherence to high-level moral principles, especially those core values and professional principles recognized and endorsed by one's organization.

MCL will test the RL's integrity. Many of the values and practices of the assembly-line school are diametrically opposed to MCL values and expectations. Learner needs replace administrative convenience. A strong learner focus replaces teacher-centered classrooms. Honesty, trust, and integrity are requirements for the RL to make this transformation.

- **Commitment:**    people's willingness to devote their full energies and talents to the successful completion of undertakings they have agreed to pursue, despite challenges and adverse conditions that may arise.

Most educators, when they learn of the MCL Vision, know that it's right, that it's highly desirable. If you don't have those beliefs, a MCL Learning Community is not where you should be. Making the transformational change to MCL is difficult even when everyone is committed. RLs are committed to that end and will surround themselves with like-minded professionals.

# PRINCIPLES OF PROFESSIONALISM OF THE RELATIONAL LEADER

- **Inclusiveness:** consistent commitment to maximizing both the range of opportunities for success available to organizational members, and the number of people included in relevant and meaningful organizational decisions.

Including those who will be impacted by a decision in the decision making process is obvious and natural for the RL. The RL believes that, "No one of us is smarter than all of us" and wants the best thinking to drive the decision. The RL also knows that we have a good "follow-through track record" when we are taking our own advice.

- **Win-Win:** a commitment to achieving and experiencing mutual benefit in the agreements people make, the relationships they establish, and the rewards they obtain from the contributions they make.

Stephen Covey suggests that win-win or lose-lose are the only options. Win-lose most frequently turns into lose-lose as the loser works to get even. No matter how messy and smelly the process of deciding comes to be, the RL thinks that there is a win-win hiding in there someplace. And there is! Finding win-win requires that the RL be thinking win-win as he is pulling out his chair to begin the discussion.

MCL makes win-win easy to accomplish. Obviously a win for learners; teachers can now think and act like the professionals they have always wanted to be, previously inhibited by the Industrial Age assembly-line structure of schools; principals can move from management to leadership; parents are happy that their children like school, and everyone can be proud of their MCL Learning Community. Well, that's how we see it anyway! Done deal, right?

# PERFORMANCE ROLES OF THE RELATIONAL LEADER

The essence of the Relational Leader is embodied in three critical performance roles:

> ▶ *Developing an open, change-friendly MCL culture*
>
> ▶ *Involving everyone in the MCL change process*
>
> ▶ *Creating meaning for everyone*

# PR 7: Developing an Open, Change-Friendly MCL Culture

This Performance Role begins with the Relational Leader's understanding and acceptance of the power of organizational culture. In short, the culture of the learning community forms a silent decision screen that, to some degree, controls the way people think, feel, communicate, and behave. Organizational culture can be a positive force for the implementation of MCL or a negative force. It can be strong or weak. It can be bureaucratic or learner-centered. RLs know that there will be organizational culture. They know that to have a culture is not a choice. The question then becomes, will we act consciously to create a MCL culture and, if so, what do we want that culture to be. The Relational Leader comes down solidly on the side of consciously creating a MCL culture and goes about involving people in determining what that culture will be. "If it's important, it should be intentional."

If your learning community has created a Strategic Design, a good place to begin is the Beliefs and Values section of the SD. What do we believe about learners and learning, what do we believe about learning facilitators and learning coaches, and what do we believe about learning communities?

> *A quick note about vocabulary:* Our personal and organizational vocabulary has a significant impact on our culture. We consciously and strategically use MCL vocabulary: "learning facilitators and learning coaches" rather than the traditional "teachers and teaching" labels in the above paragraph. Simply using these terms subtly signals a shift in our beliefs about professional roles. If we say, "students, teachers, classrooms, school, district" do you get a picture? If we say, "learners, learning facilitators, learning centers, learning community," you get a different picture. It signals or symbolizes a different culture.

## FOUR CHANGE-FRIENDLY CULTURAL NORMS

The literature we reviewed prior to the *Total Leaders* book strongly suggests that effective and successful Relational Leaders consistently work to develop cultures that have two highly visible, mutually reinforcing features. First, the culture is empowering; it promotes personal initiative, improved performance, and organizational effectiveness. Second, the culture is change friendly and openly encourages new ideas, dynamism, and lasting organizational health. Empowering Relational Leaders shape and reward four key cultural norms.

CULTURAL NORM #1: *Openness*

> Grounded in a sense of psychological security. Openness reflects a willingness and a desire to receive, consider, and act ethically on information, possibilities, and perspectives of all kinds – including "unconventional" ones.

Our sense is that educators are becoming more and more open to the need for educational reform, and *Inevitable: MCL* has led this change in thinking for many. Relational Leaders can take advantage of this movement by modeling future focusing and encouraging everyone to be students of the future. More specifically, by encouraging and expecting that everyone search for online learning opportunities for our learners, and by watching for new mass customizing technologies that might be applied to education. They are everywhere; we don't have to reinvent the wheel. (For instance, just this week we learned how a large insurance company is customizing car insurance to fit the driver's exact driving habits and basing their premiums on what they learn from the auto's black box. Your specific driving determines the cost of your insurance. Implications for education? Think a bit, they are there!)

CULTURAL NORM #2: *Innovation*

> Employees risk trying promising new ideas. They keep what works, and "let go" of what doesn't. Mistakes are opportunities for further learning, not conditions of "failure" or sources of blame.

> *"People who don't take risks*
> *generally make about two big mistakes a year.*
>
> *People who do take risks*
> *generally make about two big mistakes a year."*
>
> **Peter Drucker**

School principals have been conditioned to focus on control first and learner needs second. That focus needs to be flipped. Control is a good thing and is a must for principals. But if innovation, trying bold new ways of meeting learner needs, is to become part of the learning community culture, the learning center leaders and learning facilitators need to think first about learning and second about control. Like in, "OK, sounds great, let's try that. But I worry a bit about how we keep track of where everyone is; let's work on that, too."

Leaders need to promote innovation and risk taking, knowing that some things will work and others won't. Research regarding successful businesses (think 3M) estimate that only about 20% of their innovative attempts are successful. Eighty percent don't work. Doesn't sound like a good ratio but successful businesses quickly learn from their mistakes, drop their failed innovations and run hard with the 20% that proved to be successful. Over time, running with the successful, even though only one-fifth of their tries, makes their innovative culture well worth the risks.

Big jumps in the performance of learning communities will not happen if we are afraid to risk. We work with the lives of young people so we must be careful, we must be good planners, but we must also accept some "good shot failures." How the RL accepts failure of "good shot tries" will go a long way in determining if the learning community is to have an "innovative culture."

CULTURAL NORM #3: *Cooperation*

> Employees pool their talents and cooperate in the workplace so that they can compete successfully in the marketplace. Teaming and helping others to look good are encouraged *and celebrated*.

The Lone Ranger is dead, Vince Lombardi is gone, John Wayne is no longer with us . . . The problems of the world today tend to be more complex than they were 20 years ago, and their solutions require the expertise and experience of more than one person, no matter how capable that person may be. "No one of us is as smart as all of us" is more than a "sticky" statement. Relational Leaders involve everyone in the change process and share decisions with those impacted by the decision.

Learning communities are complex organizations with complex problems. Team problem solving is required. Learners are complex humans with complex learning needs. The expanded learning opportunities made available by teaching teams are helpful to the learner. We believe that "teaming" is good for learners, AND for learning facilitators. Teaching in our "egg crate" schools, one teacher per classroom is a lonely place for many educators. We get used to it, but at the cost of watching and learning from others, and at the cost of professional, collegial relationships.

RLs create teams and, when they can, they allow for the creation of self-selected teams. They charge those teams with implementation of the MCL Vision, but they don't micromanage. They trust teams to be learner-centered, to make team decisions, to know when things are working and when change is required, and they trust teams to continuously improve the learning opportunities for learners. RLs create and maintain a culture of cooperation, shared decision making, and teaming. And oh yes, the learning center leader should also be a member (think modeling) of a small collegial group of leaders . . . and the superintendent, well, they work with and learn from the three or four neighboring superintendents when they meet for a three-hour, agenda-driven lunch on the first Tuesday of each month.

So, RL, get creative people working together. Trust that five smart people collaborating can tackle a problem better than one person can, since they feed off each other's insights and share the risks and rewards.

CULTURAL NORM #4: *Success*

> Employees recognize that it's the norm to plan well, work hard, work smart, keep learning, and win. When they don't win after doing their best, they collectively study how not to make the same mistakes again.

Success for all is embedded in a MCL culture. First and foremost the success is for the learners. The MCL design begins with learners, and the MCL structure and systems make possible our "meeting the individual and personal learning needs of every learner, every hour, of every day" *chant.*

"Success" is for learners, YES, a no-brainer, but also success for teachers who become professional learning facilitators and learning coaches. We believe strongly that education is the world's most important profession, and that teachers/learning facilitators are "where the rubber meets the road." Make them the heroes and heroines of the learning community , , , because they are!

We can't leave this "success" dimension of the MCL culture without moving to the big education picture. Our profession sure could use, a little good news, today. We believe the MCL Vision has the power to leapfrog everything and everyone who remains committed to the Industrial Age assembly line. The MCL Vision will replace our bureaucratic structure, policies, and practices. Talk it up, Relational Leader, get others to join you, make these four cultural attributes true for your learning community and for our profession. Go for it!

## YOUR CULTURE VISION

*Should we have a vision statement about culture? Well maybe.*

Frequently good ideas remain only ideas unless we do something – like put it into writing, distribute it, refer to it whenever the opportunity arises, etc. We are visionaries and recently learned that "goals" were "visions with their work clothes on." We liked that metaphor. True and "sticky." So, RL, how about making it a short-term goal to create a one-page vision statement that could bring all of this Performance Role together? Think about a vision statement formatted much like the vision statement we used as an example in Chapter 2.

Begin with an opening statement about the power of culture, and then, in a bulleted format, identify the three to five cultural norms that you believe to be ideal for your learning community or learning center. To provide some concrete direction to your vision, it would be good if there were a one-sentence definition for each of the norms your group has chosen . . . chosen with your influence and stealth direction of course. And to give the vision teeth substance, you might list two things that people **will do** to make each specific cultural norm a reality, and one thing people **will not do** to sabotage making that norm a reality. You WILL, of course, consider one or more of the cultural aspects listed above, and it goes without saying that it is critical that you involve everyone in this visioning process. (Well maybe it doesn't "go without saying.")

## THE RL AS CULTURAL "STORYTELLER"

For some, culture is an abstract concept. Terrence Deal, in his book, *Corporate Cultures* identifies the following as "Tangible Forms of Culture:"

- Heroes and Heroines
- Rituals
- Ceremonies
- Traditions
- Symbols
- Shared Vision
- Stories

Our experience has told us the culture of a learning center or learning community can be defined by looking at:

- What you model
- What you honor
- What you accept
- What you reward
- AND, what stories are told!

When we first heard of the power of "stories" as a leadership strategy we were amused. But as the power "stories" began showing up again and again in the leadership literature, we started to take it more seriously. We are now believers and advocates in how stories drive organizational culture. And so, a few stories about culture follow:

## Culture Story: *Bayou Bob's Restaurant*

*(cjs) While having lunch at Bayou Bob's, a popular restaurant in Denver, I noticed that none of the waitstaff went back to the kitchen empty handed. They were picking up used plates from their tables but also from everyone else's tables, always hustling, never missing a beat. I asked our waitress how this "culture" of good food, fast service, cooperative and skilled workers had been established. She didn't understand the "culture" question, but looked me in the eye, smiled, and said: "That's just how we do things around here."*

*I asked her about the guy who was surveying the dining room scene while hustling around and sometimes bussing tables and she said, "Oh, that's Bob." Bob might not have understood the "culture" question either, but he had established one, one that worked for him and for his customers.*

## Culture Story: *Bully-Free Zone (for us too!)*

*(bmcg) I have been so privileged to work with incredibly gifted and committed teachers — all over the country. As we have said, THEY are our heroes and heroines. Education is a people intensive profession. I look out at audiences in various trainings and am awed by the knowledge and expertise sitting in that room. I also wonder . . . how can we tap into that expertise and share it? Many teachers silently create successful learning opportunities and structures for their learners. Often, I, or their principals, ask them to share their successes with the staff. And, equally as often, they are reticent to do so. I have wondered, "Why is that?"*

*One answer is that they find it hard to be in front of peers. I agree! However, there is another reason — perhaps the <u>real</u> reason. If or when they share their successes, many meet with "ribbing" or "teasing" from their peers. Recently, I have called it more accurately a subtle form of bullying. The response from many teachers has been overwhelming. They tell me that I have exposed a huge "elephant in the room." If we are to create a MCL Community, we must create a healthy culture of continuous improvement, of celebration and collaboration. A culture of ribbing, teasing, or subtle bullying, even in the name of humor, will stall and kill innovation. Those innovative teachers need protection and support. The power to do this lies with the Relational Leader.*

Culture Story: *No One Failing Algebra!*

*(cjs) The "school year" had officially ended a couple of days earlier, and I was walking through a high school with Bob, the HS principal, discussing construction projects for the summer. We passed a classroom door and I spotted Frank, crew cut hair, white shirt, bow tie and jacket at a blackboard with one student sitting in the front row . . . no one else in the room. Frank was using his traditional tools, chalk and blackboard, to explain an algebra problem. The scene looked a bit odd given that the school year was over. I didn't disturb the teacher / learner activity in the room, but a couple of steps past the door I leaned over and said, "Hey Bob, what the hell was that?" Bob said, "Oh, that's Frank. No one in his 20 years with us has ever failed Algebra . . . and that kid sure as hell won't be the first!"*

*Good story, good humor, fun to tell. But it was more than "just a story." It was a statement of Frank's values and the culture of his department and his school and a culture that I wanted to permeate the entire district. Frank and Bob did not accept failure; if the kid hadn't met the Algebra standards, he had not failed . . . he just wasn't finished yet.*

*The story was told over and over again with Frank always the hero. No new teacher to the district could miss the message, "We have standards and we don't accept failure." I was one of the storytellers.*

Stories are powerful. Relational Leaders work at being good storytellers.

The culture of the learning community is destined to be a reflection of the RL's personal values and principles. <u>Your</u> behaviors (*what you say, what you do, AND how you say and do what you say and do*) create the culture. It is created by:

- who you choose to recognize and what you recognize them for,
- who you help to make heroines and heroes,
- what you will and won't accept,
- who you hire and who you outcounsel,
- what you reward and who you reward,
- who gets team leader positions, and
- who is asked to present at the MCL Conference.

These are opportunities to influence your ideal culture, so be conscious of <u>what</u> you do and <u>how</u> you do it. Remember: you ARE the culture of your learning community.

No matter what, THERE WILL BE CULTURE! But, YOU get a choice in the culture you are creating.

116

---

### ORGANIZATIONAL CULTURES can be

| | | |
|---|---|---|
| *Strong* | *or* | *Weak* |
| *Aligned* | *or* | *Opposed* |
| *Helpful* | *or* | *Harmful* |
| *Clear* | *or* | *Fuzzy* |
| *Overt* | *or* | *Covert* |
| *Functional* | *or* | *Dysfunctional* |
| *Deliberate* | *or* | *Happenstance* |
| *Flexible* | *or* | *Bureaucratic* |

---

# PR 8: Involving Everyone in the MCL Change Process

Who should the Relational Leader involve in the change process? Anyone and everyone who will be impacted by the change – and involved from the earliest point possible. In the case of a learning community, the list of "stakeholders" is extensive and definitely includes learners, their parents, their relatives, and their neighbors – any of whom might eventually be found discussing the MCL Vision while selecting vegetables at the local Safeway. Do you want them to know what you are doing and why? Do you want them to support the change whenever the topic comes up? Well, Yes, and Yes. So if you are wondering "if they" should be involved, they should.

## WHY INVOLVE PEOPLE?

Why this heavy involvement in the change process? When we ask that question when working with leadership groups, the first answer we usually get is, "Well, if you want people committed to the change, you had better involve them in the change process." Hooray! It's a no-brainer, and everyone agrees! But if we wait just a bit and let the question hang in front of the group, someone will invariably suggest that, "You might also get a good idea or two from the people who will have to understand and do the changing." Great, both responses are good reasons for widespread involvement. But which reason would the RL suggest first? And why? (Please stop here to consider your response before continuing.)

---

### **WHY** involve people???

| | |
|---|---|
| Wisdom: | *None of us is as smart as all of us* |
| Education: | *We all learn while doing* |
| Communication: | *I already know about it* |
| Change Friendly: | *Well, yes, I'm part of the change culture here* |
| Safety: | *We share the burden and the joy* |
| Strategy: | *Along the way, we learned about the roadblocks and resources* |

---

We think that the RL would involve people because she sincerely believes that they have much to offer, which emanates from her No. 1 Value: _Integrity_. Simply involving people just to get their "buy in" can be viewed as manipulative and *not* acting with integrity, which, in turn, fosters suspicion and resentment. Integrity demands openness and honesty. Inclusiveness demands trust and high expectations of the participants.

## CREATING A SAFE PLACE

For many, change is fearful and something to avoid because it too frequently comes across as "what those people want us to do." In education, this is often called "fixing the teachers" . . . but leaving the rest of the system untouched. Relational Leaders are able to avoid or modify this condition because of their ability to see change from the perspective of the learning facilitators and the learners. RLs see real change as a process that happens from the inside out, starting with the paradigm perspectives, beliefs, values, and goals of the people affected. They know that when people begin to see things differently through new eyes and paradigms, and when they begin to feel psychologically safe, they can open up emotionally to explore the MCL Vision.

Relational Leaders create this safe place by helping others openly address questions about:

### **Their psychological readiness for change**:
- *How secure do I feel as a person and as a member of this learning community?*
- *How does the MCL Vision fit with my personal values?*
- *What's in it for me?*
- *Is the potential reward worth the obvious risk?*
- *Do I have the skills and abilities to do MCL?*

**The organization's culture:**
- *Are the heroes/heroines in our learning community innovators and risk takers?*
- *What happens around here to people who try new things and fail?*
- *What happens to those who try new things and succeed? Are our leaders people we can trust?*

**The organization's structure:**
- *What happened to the last major change effort tried by our learning community?*
- *Is the leadership of the learning community willing to change its structures and "way of doing business" to accomplish the MCL Vision?*
- *Can we trust our leaders to take the risks to significantly change the fundamental way we do things?*

With a safe psychological place established, RLs are better able to recruit, include, and involve all of the learning community's members in the exploration and implementation of the MCL Vision.

# PR 9: Creating Meaning for Everyone Through the MCL Vision

Involving people in the change process gets them thinking differently. It creates different and clearer expectations; it creates excitement and meaning. Their work with learners and their personal missions become more meaningful for everyone.

Ken Robinson in his great book titled *The Element: How Finding You Passion Changes Everything,* helped us to clarify and articulate something that we intuitively have always known.

> *"Happiness and success are the result of finding*
> *The point at which our passion and our natural talents intersect."*
>
> Our paraphrase of **Ken Robinson**

We believe that there is no profession as meaningful as education; nothing more important in our lives than creating life-long learners; nothing more meaningful than to transform education into the image of the MCL Vision. Where our natural talents lie might be in question, but our passion is evident. What could be more important than education! *That's not a question BTW, it is our statement.*

We begin the "Meaning" Performance Role with Ken Robinson's statement because we want to influence you when making your most important decision as a Total Leader. What is that most important decision? Do we have your attention! The most important decision you make is:

*Who you hire to be learning facilitators and learning coaches.*

The impact of that decision is awesome. Your hire will impact as many as 100 young learners every year. Multiply that number times the number of years we hope to keep him in the profession. Bottom line . . . don't hire anyone who doesn't have a passion for learning and learners. If they think there is another profession more important, wish them well. We can help people learn the skills of the learning facilitator/learning coach, but we can't teach meaning and passion. Be blunt and direct in the interview process. Ask straight out, "Do you believe that education is the most important profession?" No "spin" allowed.

## Six Key "Meaning Makers"

Relational Leaders are creators and promoters of meaning, and meaning emanates out of:

- "Belonging," and
- Doing things of value.

Here's where Relational Leaders in education have an enormous head start due to the profession's intrinsic value. If empowering children and young adults to lead happy and successful lives doesn't have meaning, then what does? If shaping and encouraging the world's next generation of leaders isn't valuable, then what is? Meaning is everywhere in education, and Relational Leaders never lose sight of it. Consequently, they understand and continuously communicate that meaning comes from six key things:

1. **A compelling purpose:** We humans find meaning in doing work that is significant, makes a difference in the lives of others, and we personally feel passionate about. All work has purpose and meaning, but education work is top drawer. Thoughtful and caring leaders identify and communicate that meaning whenever and however possible. Meaningful work leads to motivation, motivation leads to engagement, and engagement leads to excellence and productivity. Relational Leaders never allow educating children to become "just another job." We are in the business of "Empowering ALL Learners to

Succeed in a Rapidly Changing World." (We were about to add, "and that ain't kid stuff," but it really IS "kid stuff.")

2. **Seeing and being part of the big picture:** We humans find meaning in doing work that is part of something lasting and bigger than ourselves. Does the bricklayer think of his work as laying bricks, building walls, or constructing a cathedral? Each level of perception elevates the work's meaning and creates a corresponding level of motivation. We're betting that the bricklayer who's constructing cathedrals is more engaged in, committed to, and fulfilled in his work than his other two counterparts. The MCL Vision ranks as "the big picture" of education.

3. **Meeting challenges and high expectations:** Meaning comes from accomplishing challenging tasks and meeting high expectations. If work is routine that anyone can do, there's little "significance" or deeper meaning in it. This can be a key motivator for educators, and Relational Leaders know how to work with it. Challenge is everywhere in education, and parents and the public have high expectations for their highly diverse children. Recall that we suggested "everyone must know how the MCL Vision will affect them personally." Well, this is where the challenge and high expectations should show up.

4. **Being in control and responsible:** If being in control and responsible sounds like being empowered, it should. When someone else lays out our work, tells us how and when to do it, and we don't produce, we can easily dismiss the results as "not our fault." But when we take on the responsibility to do the work and the leader puts us in control of the resources we need to do it, we take pride in our abilities, our accomplishments, and ourselves. We live in the Age of Empowerment and everyone should be in control of the things that will ensure their contribution to the implementation of the MCL Vision.

5. **Being part of a team:** For most of us, "winning" at something – doing it with excellence and flair as an individual – is fun. But "winning" as a team is multi-dimensional fun. When professional golfers win a tournament, there is jubilation for a moment or so, but the winners soon retreat back into their previous reserve and composure. They check and sign their scorecard and submit to the TV interviews with little emotion. But watch a close basketball game and you'll see the winning team and their fans

shouting, hugging, waving towels, and carrying on. Identifying with, and being part of, a recognizable team is emotionally energizing and meaningful. Relational Leaders deliberately work to create teams and bring them together to win as a team.

6. **Feedback/keeping track:** Ken Blanchard is right when he says "feedback is the breakfast of champions." Without some form of keeping track, or keeping score, how can anyone know how well they're doing? And without knowing how well they are doing, how can they work toward continuous improvement? Relational Leaders create feedback loops that help their people see how well they're doing. They know that keeping track creates meaning, that meaning enhances productivity, and that being productive in an important endeavor creates meaning. It's a perfect, non-vicious, empowering cycle.

Relational Leaders believe that today's Age of Empowerment is a great time to be leading and that the MCL Vision could not have arrived at a more opportune time. They recognize that helping people find meaning in their work is the result of the culture in which they work and the involvement they have in shaping the direction and substance of that work. Both bring meaning to people's lives and directly benefit the organization as well. Education is full of opportunities for creating and experiencing meaning; and Relational Leaders really lay that groundwork as they gear up for launching and sustaining the MCL Vision.

Moreover, RLs are basically nice people. You might recognize them by simply asking yourself, "Who do I like being with at work? Who makes me feel like a contributor? Who do I trust enough to be candid with about controversial issues?" And while RLs aren't all alike, they do have important things in common: they're humble, secure, candid, relatively ego-free, capable, courageous, honest, reflective, collaborative, and *productive.*

## REFLECTION: ASSESS AND PLAN

The following self-assessment rubrics (Figures 5.1 – 5.4) might help you to reflect on your knowledge and skills related to *The Relational MCL Leader* and to focus your professional development.

**Reflection Question 1 (Relational Leadership)**

| I. SELF ASSESS<br>(How am I doing?) | What is the degree to which I<br>understand Relational Leadership? |
|---|---|
| 4  INNOVATING | *I can help others understand the role of Relational Leadership, its function within the Total Leaders Framework, how it is necessary for productive change.* |
| 3  APPLYING | *I seek feedback on and reflect on how I am doing as a Relational Leader.* |
| 2  DEVELOPING | *I can explain the values, Principles of Professionalism, and Performance Roles of Relational Leadership.* |
| 1  BEGINNING | *I can identify the characteristics, the mindset, and examples of Relational Leadership.* |

| II. PLAN FOR IMPROVEMENT<br>(What do I need to do?) | III. SUPPORT RESOURCES<br>(Where can I get help?) |
|---|---|
| *What are strategies that I will use to improve my understanding of Relational Leadership?* | *What and/or who are resources that will help me to improve my understanding of Relational Leadership?* |

**Figure 5.1**

**Reflection Question 2 (Relational Leadership)**

| I. SELF ASSESS<br>(How am I doing?) | What is the degree to which I<br>develop an open, change-friendly MCL culture? |
|---|---|
| 4  INNOVATING | *I am the lead story-teller of examples of our MCL Vision.* |
| 3  APPLYING | *I strategically create and honor tangible forms of culture which reflect our MCL Vision (heroes, heroines, rituals, ceremonies, traditions).* |
| 2  DEVELOPING | *I led the creation of a vision of our preferred culture with 3-5 cultural norms.* |
| 1  BEGINNING | *I can identify the characteristics of and norms of an empowering, change-friendly MCL culture.* |

| II. PLAN FOR IMPROVEMENT<br>(What do I need to do?) | III. SUPPORT RESOURCES<br>(Where can I get help?) |
|---|---|
| *What are strategies that I will use to develop an open, change-friendly MCL culture?* | *What and/or who are resources that will help me to develop an open, change-friendly MCL culture?* |

**Figure 5.2**

**Reflection Question 3 (Relational Leadership)**

| I. SELF ASSESS (How am I doing?) | What is the degree to which I involve everyone in the MCL change process? |
|---|---|
| 4  INNOVATING | I help others to understand the "WIIFYs"(what's in it for you) for each stakeholder group in making our MCL Vision a reality. |
| 3  APPLYING | I create formal and informal structures to involve stakeholders in making the MCL Vision a reality. |
| 2  DEVELOPING | I create a safe psychological place by openly addressing questions of stakeholders about our MCL Vision. |
| 1  BEGINNING | I involve people in the change process because I sincerely believe that they have much to offer and that real change happens from the inside out. |

| II. PLAN FOR IMPROVEMENT (What do I need to do?) | III. SUPPORT RESOURCES (Where can I get help?) |
|---|---|
| What are strategies that I will use to involve everyone in the MCL change process? | What and/or who are resources that will help me to involve everyone in the MCL change process? |

**Figure 5.3**

## Reflection Question 4 (Relational Leadership)

| I. SELF ASSESS (How am I doing?) | What is the degree to which I create meaning everyone in our MCL Vision? |
|---|---|
| 4 INNOVATING | *I help others to understand that the Information Age has given way to the Age of Empowerment. Empowerment fuels meaning.* |
| 3 APPLYING | *I help all stakeholders to find their personal meaning in our MCL Vision.* |
| 2 DEVELOPING | *I openly communicate my value of having everyone find meaning in the MCL work and that meaning comes from belonging and doing things of value.* |
| 1 BEGINNING | *I reinforce — constantly — the importance of our role: to create life-long learners; to transform education into the MCL Vision.* |

| II. PLAN FOR IMPROVEMENT (What do I need to do?) | III. SUPPORT RESOURCES (Where can I get help?) |
|---|---|
| *What are strategies that I will do to create meaning for everyone in our MCL Vision?* | *What and/or who are resources that will help me to create meaning for everyone in our MCL Vision?* |

**Figure 5.4**

# Chapter 6

# The Quality Leader

*Shaping Up!*

| | Profile of<br><br>**THE**<br>**QUALITY EDUCATIONAL LEADER**<br><br>*Leading Competently and Expertly* |
|---|---|
| MINDSET | All learners have the right to be empowered to succeed when they leave our learning community. We will implement a set of life role learner outcomes that all learners will demonstrate and make part of their ePortfolio. |
| PURPOSE | To establish expectations, procedures, and practices that guarantee the continuous improvement of learner results, and the processes for achieving those results. |
| CHANGE BELIEF | Change happens when individuals and teams have the capacity to implement the learning community's MCL Vision. We are here to help our people create that capacity. |
| PERFORMANCE ROLES | ▶ Develops and empowers the learning community's staff<br>▶ Creates, applies, and uses feedback loops<br>▶ Improves the learning community's performance |
| PERSONAL VALUES | Excellence<br>Productivity |
| PRINCIPLES | Accountability<br>Improvement |
| THE GURU<br>THE EXEMPLAR<br>KEY SOURCES: | W. Edwards Deming<br>Steve Jobs, former Apple CEO<br><br>• *Strength-Based Leadership,* Tom Rath and Barry Conchie, 2008<br>• *Good to Great,* Jim Collins, 2001<br>• *Now Discover Your Strengths,* Marcus Buckingham and Donald Clifton, 2004<br>• *The Element: How Finding Your Passion Changes Everything,* Ken Robinson, 2009<br>• *Mindset: The New Psychology of Success,* Carol S. Dweck, 2007<br>• *Drive: The Surprising Truth About What Motivates Us,* Daniel Pink, 2011 |

# THE QUALITY LEADER

## *Creates the Capacity to Implement the MCL Vision*

*"Be a yardstick of quality. Some people aren't
used to an environment where excellence is expected."*

**Steve Jobs**

**ALERT: HEAVY LIFTING!** With this Leadership Domain, the Total Leader takes us directly to the right side of the TL Framework. We are now about *Strategic Alignment*; we are now into the "heavy lifting" part of the Leadership/Management continuum. To refresh your memory, let us again flash the Total Leaders 101 visual.

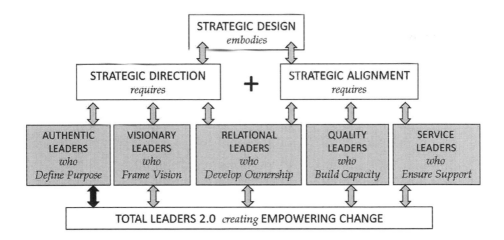

**Figure 6.1**

# QUALITY: THE TICKET TO THE GAME

When you get a new car you expect everything to work. When you get a new Surface tablet, you expect new features and smooth operations. Well, the MCL Vision is the new, new thing. We have designed everything to work, which is to say that we have aligned all of the Performance Roles with the MCL Vision. We expect the Performance Roles of the Quality Leader and the Service Leader to tell you what needs to be done if you are going to have a smooth grand opening of the vision. The first PR for the Quality Leader will have to do with creating and using feedback loops. Feedback loops are about strategic alignment. When we have aligned people, policies, and practices with our vision, we can expect an organization that is both effective and efficient. We need to be in tune with and conscious of the efficiencies that can be created in the learning community when we are in full Strategic Alignment.

> *"Leadership is the capacity to translate vision into reality."*
>
> **Warren Bennis**

Joel Barker, in his famous "The Business of Paradigms" video, boldly stated "The quality paradigm is the most pervasive shift of the past 20 years." Where has all of that gone? Don't hear much about Total Quality Management (TQM) these days. What happened? Well, it hasn't gone away. It is now _assumed_. Quality is table stakes, the ticket to the game.

Educators and the education profession have been in trouble in the "Quality Domain." We have been reluctant to be accountable for learners learning. Politicians didn't like that, and created their own crude and wrong form of accountability. You do remember No Child Left Behind, don't you!? Politicians grabbed onto the only way they knew to measure student achievement, achievement test scores, and gave us high-stakes testing which, for many, has become the total focus of education. *How sad.*

Let us retreat somewhat on this accusation about educators not being account-able and not providing quality. Educators and educational leaders as a whole are good, moral people who work hard and do what they think is right for learners. There are a couple of aspects of education for which educators have always been accountable. First, they are accountable for a quality **context** for learning. Learners in many cases are treated with more caring and dignity at school than anywhere else, including their homes. We have libraries full of books, good food service, buses that are safe and clean.

The **context for learning,** for the most part, is of high quality. Many school accreditation processes focus on quality in the context of learning.

Second, educators have also been accountable for **processes,** for how we do what we do. Teachers know how to teach ala Madeline Hunter, albeit how to teach in an Industrial Age school. Principals are typically good managers. Schools run efficiently. The processes of "having school" are smooth and efficient; they are of quality.

However, there is a third, and most critical aspect of educational accountability that has been avoided: **product** accountability, that is, learner **achievement.** Do learners learn what is taught? Learners learning IS the product, the service, the reason for education. Educators have argued that, "learning is too complex to measure, that low achievement is highly correlated with poverty and parenting, etc." This point of view has some validity.

Today's schools are mostly time-based. We have all heard the "one liner," "Time is the constant and learning is the variable" when someone is zeroing in on what is wrong with the assembly-line delivery of instruction. MCL makes learning the outcome and time the variable. W. Edwards Deming, icon of the "Quality Paradigm," would turn over in his grave to know that we still give learners B and C grades in Algebra at the end of the semester. By doing so, "good enough" trumps quality.

*Don't give the learner a "B-" for Algebra. A "B-" indicates*
*that she "isn't finished with Algebra, YET!"*

Do educators not value quality? Now, we know that they DO care, darn it . . . but not enough to change the structure of schools (e.g the grading system) so that every learner taking Algebra leaves the course being able to demonstrate all Algebra learner outcomes. Whose fault is it that we do not change the structures? *Well, it's not the teacher's.*

Leaders have the power to make the structural changes that make the MCL Vision doable. In fairness to leaders, the learner/teacher ratio and the absence of technology have limited options to the assembly line, and those options have been of the "tinkering" variety. That reality changed significantly with the mass customization breakthroughs that make MCL doable. Everyone needs to be involved in a change process of this magnitude, but the leader must "take the lead."

Dr. Bill Spady's work with learner outcomes, outcomes written in the form of learner "demonstrations of learning," makes objective measures of learning possible which, in turn, makes quality learning and system accountability possible. Learners, educators, and parents should embrace the breakthrough. Place MCL between the learner outcome and the objective assessment, add an electronic portfolio to document the learning demonstration, and we have the learning system that makes proof of quality learning and accountability a reality. When we do that, we will again focus on what is important for learners to learn and, hopefully, regain control of our profession.

## QUALITY AND MASS CUSTOMIZED LEARNING

Quality Leadership is about developing organizational and staff capacity to change and improve, to make the MCL Vision doable. Remember, people and organizations don't change:

- unless there is a compelling reason to change (Authentic Leader Domain),
- unless they have a clear picture of that change (Visionary Leader Domain),
- unless they are committed to making the change (Relational Leader Domain).

But even then, people and organizations cannot change unless they have the _capacity_ to do so – the fourth of our *Pillars of Change*. Quality leaders have the mindset and abilities to stimulate employees to grow and develop as people and to establish ever-higher expectations and standards for the MCL instructional delivery system, for learner learning opportunities, and for the quality of learning results.

Deming was the most noted of all the quality gurus, and he believed strongly that the organization itself is the major part of any production problem. He demonstrated that workers could and would change if quality programs started at the top and leaders implemented the kinds of organizational processes that strengthened and supported workers' abilities. Originally Deming claimed that around 85 percent of the functional and quality problems in any organization are caused by the organization itself, and the workers cause only about 15 percent of the problems. Later in his career, he changed those figures to 94 and 6 percent respectively.

The quality paradigm is a critical element/principle of MCL and is built into the vision from the start. Surely learner learning deserves at least as much quality emphasis as does a Lexus! We have high expectations that our people and our profession will create the capacity to meet the learning needs of every learner every hour of every day. Our assembly-line structure will be replaced by mass customizing technology and the roles and responsibilities of the learning facilitators and learning coaches will also change in significant ways. The QL will be challenged in building the capacity for the new vision, but it will be so worth it. We believe that MCL will happen and spread quickly once it takes off. The promise and desirability of the MCL Vision makes it, well, *Inevitable*. We hope and trust that *Inevitable Too!* will help the QL make it doable.

# MORAL FOUNDATION OF THE QUALITY LEADER

The values of excellence and productivity and the principles of accountability and improvement couldn't fit this Leadership Domain and Pillar of Change any better. The Quality Leader is charged with Strategic Alignment as outlined in the learning community's Strategic Design. He is charged with aligning people (himself included), processes, policies and structures with the MCL Vision. His values and principles speak to that alignment. He is charged with getting everyone and everything pulling in the MCL Vision direction. No wasted energy or wasted resources allowed.

# VALUES OF THE QUALITY LEADER

- **Excellence:** a desire for, and pursuit of, the highest quality in any undertaking, process, product, or result

For Quality Leaders, excellence and quality are synonyms. By this standard, if your work is not what you would label and judge as your best, you haven't finished yet. The role of today's teacher is difficult, without doubt. New learning facilitator roles will be equally difficult, but we believe that those roles will be much more professional, meaningful, and satisfying.

- **Productivity:** the optimum use of available time, resources, technologies and talent to achieve desired results.

We want to get things done as well as enjoy doing them. The MCL Vision comes with that built in . . . for the staff and for the learners. Quality Leaders value accomplishment, achievement, and getting things done – well and on time! That too fits both the staff and the MCL learner.

# PRINCIPLES OF PROFESSIONALISM OF THE QUALITY LEADER

- **Accountability:** taking responsibility for the content and the process of decisions made, actions taken, and the resulting outcomes.

Quality Leaders openly and comfortably take responsibility for themselves and for their team. They embrace accountability for learner learning. They volunteer rather than duck, and solve problems rather than place blame. They know that they have the opportunity to transform education; they see the possibilities and power of the MCL Vision and they go for it!

- **Improvement:** a commitment to continuously enhance the quality of personal and organizational performance, the processes used to generate results, and the results themselves.

Quality Leaders know and accept that "quality" is transitory and an ever-moving target. Today's "outstanding" will become tomorrow's "good." Joel Barker, paradigm shift guru, warns that, "When the paradigm shifts, everyone goes back to zero," and it's a new game. Singapore and South Korea, who do Industrial Age schools just as well as anyone, will be leapfrogged by MCL. That's our bet anyway. Make it yours!

# PERFORMANCE ROLE OF THE QUALITY LEADER

Quality leadership is shaped through consistent attention to three critical Performance Roles, each of which helps drive learning community alignment:

▶ *Developing and empowering everyone to implement the MCL Vision*

▶ *Creating and using feedback loops to assess MCL systems and processes*

▶ *Continually improving learning community performance*

## PR 10: Developing and Empowering Everyone to Implement the MCL Vision

Empowerment is happening even as we are writing this book. Teachers are becoming learning facilitators and learning coaches. Principals are becoming Total Leaders.

(bmcg) *I am seeing something different . . . very different. It is both exciting and sad. Let me first say that I have worked with incredibly gifted and motivated teachers all over the country. They study a new program or curriculum with commitment. They implement it with fidelity. We have groomed teachers — like our good students — to follow directions and do what the program or curriculum says to do.*

*Creating a MCL learning community, however, is different. It is not a program to "implement." It is a vision to create. This is a foreign concept for many educators. Agreeing with the vision, they immediately take on the role of dutiful implementer. They ask, "how do we" questions, expecting the answers are outside of themselves.*

*"How do we group learners differently?" "How will we allow learners to go at their own pace?" "How will we create customized learning opportunities for learners?" "How will we share the load?" "How will we use technology to . . . ?" Or, as good "do-bees," they say, "Just tell us what you want us to do." I have come to understand that we have buried teachers' sense of efficacy. We have conditioned them to think that someone else — besides them (!) — has the answer. How very sad.*

*Just as in a classroom, when I ask open-ended questions of 12 year-olds, my response to the "how do we" questions causes pause and perhaps frustration. "I don't know, how <u>will</u> we?" Wait time is important here! It takes a while . . .Yet, with patience and support, while holding tight on the vision, **IT** happens: teacher empowerment. I have never seen it before. Again, I have seen compliant, committed, hard-working teachers. This is very different. When we help teachers to see this compelling, doable, needed vision, AND unleash them, they become empowered and invested in the work. It is exciting and it's about time that we tapped our best resource.*

*The work of MCL is an inside job. It requires teams of teachers to work together — share the load — to change and create the structures to make customized learning a reality. This is different from just doing what the new vocabulary program, for example, says to do.*

We find a message in this story: *believe in the efficacy of our people, especially in the efficacy of our learning facilitators.* They are developing because they have been empowered to do so. We are seeing that when our professional colleagues "get" the MCL Vision, complete with its powerful rationale, they know what to do and pretty much how to do it. Truth is, they have always wanted to do MCL but didn't have the technological support to make it work.

When principals allow teaching teams to design the structure of their team and the roles of team members, teachers working together become great sources of "staff development" for each other. A teacher moving from the lonely role of a "classroom" teacher to a dynamic collegial team has positive implications for learners and positive implications for staff development. When we first created the Total Leaders Framework and identified the critical Performance Roles of the leader, we thought of staff development as distinctively different from "empowerment." Both had to do with building and increasing capacity to accomplish the organization's vision, but beyond that, not very related. We now understand that staff development and empowerment cannot be separated. They mesh and they are complementary. Add *teaming*, where professionals have the opportunity to work with and in front of their peers, to the strong development/empowerment combo, and you have a synergistic, capacity building powerhouse . . . all working together, friction free, and inexpensively.

## DEVELOPMENT: FROM FIXING TO SUPPORT

As we put our thoughts into writing the above paragraph, it was hard for us to say, and to think, "staff development." The term sounds so . . . *Industrial Age* . . . like "we, your leaders, are responsible for developing you, for *fixing* you." What we wanted to say was, "professional development." That term sounds more like, "you are in control of your professionalism, how might we support you." Let's see how that vocabulary change works as we write the remainder of this Performance Role. We may be on to something that will change our thinking about ~~staff development~~ professional development.

We begin this section with beliefs at the core of Gallup's research on effective leadership. Their work is labeled the "Strengths Movement" and captured in Figure 6.2.

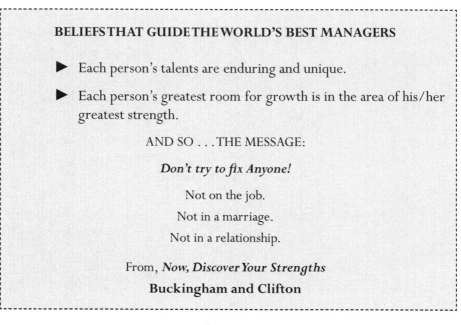

**BELIEFS THAT GUIDE THE WORLD'S BEST MANAGERS**

► Each person's talents are enduring and unique.

► Each person's greatest room for growth is in the area of his/her greatest strength.

AND SO . . . THE MESSAGE:

*Don't try to fix Anyone!*

Not on the job.

Not in a marriage.

Not in a relationship.

From, *Now, Discover Your Strengths*
**Buckingham and Clifton**

**Figure 6.2**

These game changing beliefs have big-time implications for professional development. It moves the leader from Ms. Fixit to Ms. Empowerer, and moves the learning facilitator from, "how can I learn things that I'm just not very good at," to "what are the major contributions I can make to my team." We highly recommend the Strengths Movement approach.

# CHARACTERISTICS OF QUALITY PROFESSIONAL DEVELOPMENT:

▶ Focuses on the capacity to implement the learning community's MCL Vision. This requires leaders and teachers to fully understand the new roles of the teacher: learning facilitator and learning coach. (See the roles in the next section.)

▶ Aligns with the reward system. Rewards can take many forms (more in Chapter 7), many of which are cost free (recognition, advancement, leader positions, conference attendance) and, of course, there is always the dollar reward.

▶ Considers the characteristics of the adult learner. We adults, like our learners, have learning styles, interests, etc.; we also have obligations outside of our main work.

▶ Includes a "coaching" component. It's one thing to know what we are to do, but yet another to do it. Simply observing a MCL learning facilitator or watching a MCL team at work with learners is usually very helpful.

▶ Is facilitated by the learning community's MCL heroes and heroines. Those brave souls who were first to successfully take on the new role of learning facilitator/learning coach will have great credibility with their colleagues.

Professional growth is a personal and learning community responsibility. Today's fast changing world in which we frequently change jobs and careers requires individuals to be current in the job market, ready for their next opportunity. And, one of the characteristics of the "professional" is that he keeps up with the newest new thing. We expect our people to be life-long learners, to take responsibility for much of their professional development.

## LEARNING FACILITATORS AND LEARNING COACHES

The MCL Vision suggests roles for learning facilitators and learning coaches that are significantly different, more professional, and more rewarding than the roles of teachers today. MCL asks that we move our focus from curriculum to learners. Curriculum remains important of course but, with MCL, the learner becomes everyone's primary focus *right from the start*.

Our professional educators, those who work directly with learners, play two general roles in the MCL Vision. They are LEARNING FACILITATORS who provide direct instruction, create and deliver seminars, help individual learners through learner outcomes, supervise projects, etc. Much like teachers do today. They are also LEARNING COACHES who advise, guide, and coach individual learners. Because these roles are significantly different in most of today's schools, they will be an important focus for professional development activities. Each role is further defined below.

## TEACHER AS LEARNING FACILITATOR:

- Teaches those learner outcomes that are "best learned" via direct instruction. A significant number of outcomes, those requiring complex reasoning and application of skills, need face-to-face, direct instruction from a learning facilitator.
- Engages and inspires each learner. The learning facilitator embodies the cultural norm that everyone gets learners actively engaged in their learning.
- Creates, monitors, and supervises learning activities. Learner outcomes will drive learning opportunities. Sometimes learner outcomes will require projects, group problem solving, a mentoring arrangement with community professionals, etc. There will be a need for numerous learning activities to meet the needs of learners. For example, a learning facilitator may design a learning activity that helps learners create a business plan that meets the loan requirements of the community bank.
- Ensures that all learners effectively use the learning center's learning tools to accomplish their outcomes. We all know how "to do school," we learned that in first grade. MCL is a bit more complex than a single classroom where a teacher tells you what to do. Everyone is responsible for helping learners to manage and manipulate the new MCL system.
- Creates and delivers seminars that allow learners to accomplish complex learner outcomes. Seminars, flexible as to topic, structure, and time, will constitute a large and important part of the instructional delivery system. Seminars will be at the center of learning opportunities for every age group, but will be most important for the middle school and high school age learners.
- Along with other learning facilitators, continuously improves the learning experience and effectiveness of the learning community.

# TEACHER AS LEARNING COACH:

- Advises and mentors 15 – 18 learners. Learning coaches are the main contact between the learner, her parents or guardians and the learning center. Coaches will work with individual learners over a significant timeframe, maybe from 3 to 4 years, allowing for deep relationship building. This is a new role for many and some clear expectations will have to be developed. In-house guidance and counseling professionals may provide leadership and training to prepare the staff for this coaching role.

- Examines options and expectations for each learner. Learners take more and more responsibility for their own learning plans as they move through the system. Athletic coaches are motivators. Our learning coaches are motivators as well.

- Analyzes the learner's learning plan. Learners will eventually take responsibility for their learning, but the adult learning coach will hold the learner accountable when necessary. MCL's goal is to graduate life-long learners including strong habits of mind (e.g. self-directedness, work ethic).

- Communicates openly among and between the learner, his parents, and the learning community. The role of the coach here is to keep everyone informed of how things are going for the learner . . . and to seek support from parents and the community when problems arise.

- Along with other learning coaches, adjusts the programs and procedures in the learning community to meet the ever-changing needs of their learners. Quality Leaders and learning coaches are always looking for ways to make the system more effective and efficient for learners.

MCL is a vision, a vision that is being clarified by those who are beginning to implement the vision. The activities of the learning facilitator and coach will no doubt change and be refined with experience. Certainly the MCL Vision is a challenging undertaking. Challenging, but also rewarding.

# EMPOWERMENT: THE KEY TO INCREASING CAPACITY

Before we get into the specifics of "empowerment," let's see how it fits into the big learning community picture. Figure 6.3 is aptly labeled *The Empowerment Sequence*.

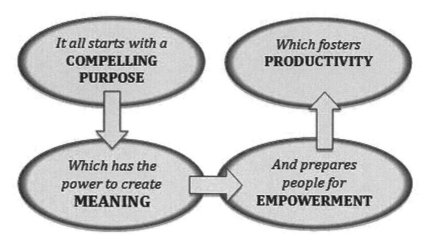

**Figure 6.3**

The four ovals are connected and interdependent. The Authentic Leader got us started when she involved the learning community in the Strategic Design process. Setting a Strategic Direction focused first on identifying a *Compelling Purpose for the Learning Community*. Stated in the form of a mission statement, it might read, "Empowering ALL Learners to Succeed in a Rapidly Changing World."

Empowering every kid! WOW, that's why I became a teacher! I want to make this happen. I want to be part of this mission. The purpose of the school district was not to continue to "have school." "Meaning," the second oval, charges our intrinsic motivation to want to make a difference in our world. *Meaning motivates!*

If I understand and value the learning community's compelling purpose and MCL Vision, and I am highly motivated, I am a strong candidate to be "empowered," and trusted to be put in control of how I do what I do. The natural end is that when we find meaning in our work and are trusted to make our own decisions, we work hard, work smart, and work long to accomplish big important things.

A Little Story (*bmcg*): *A district leader shared the following exchange she had with a veteran teacher who is a member of a team working to implement MCL. It was a few months into the school year when she exclaimed to the district leader, "This is the best year I have had teaching!" "What has made it so?" asked the district leader. The teacher paused — thought — and replied, "I feel that I am trusted."*

*This story relates to my reflection early on in this chapter. When teachers ask me "how will we" questions, I follow up my "I don't know, how will we?" response with, "I trust you." At first, they are taken aback. Very sad. But once they know I really mean it, something magical happens. Empowerment!*

In short, empowerment leads to productivity. Today's businesses know that if they fail to empower their people, they will not be able to compete. Although our product is "learners demonstrating learner outcomes" rather than apps for iPhones, the ovals are the same. And where could anyone find anything more meaningful than coaching future life-long learners? Empowerment is not a buzz word. It is the key to building capacity.

Empowerment isn't usually bestowed on someone in a flash. It's not like being "Knighted" by the Queen, being made CEO of Yahoo.com, or being selected as Miss America.

Not everyone is ready to be empowered. To be empowered one has to have a certain level of what we call "maturity." Ken Blanchard and Paul Hersey created a Situational Leadership Model. The model attaches levels of maturity with leadership interventions. It is a great leadership tool, and still relevant after many years. The maturity scales work very well when determining readiness for empowerment. People in learning communities are mature when they:

1. Are able to set high, yet attainable goals.
2. Are able to take responsibility.
3. Are willing to take responsibility.
4. Have task relevant education and/or experience.

It is interesting to see what happens when you tell people the/your criteria for being "mature." Those who do not set goals and those not willing to take responsibility suddenly become quite mature on those two scales. Ability to take responsibility comes with expertise and experience, and task relevant education, for educators, comes through their BS degree, professional development, and personal learning. Our experience is that most of today's learning facilitators are ready to be empowered. We see empowered learning facilitators whenever we get into a learning community that is working to implement the MCL Vision.

Again, empowerment isn't an all-or-nothing thing. Quality Leaders challenge learning facilitators with high expectations, but they are careful not to put teams or individuals on a project that is over their heads.

## *You have "empowerment:"*

✓  *When* . . . The purpose/mission of the learning community is clear and compelling; when the MCL Vision is clear and described in concrete terms; and when educators have embraced the learning community's vision. (Another look at the ovals in Figure 6.3 might be helpful.)

✓  *When* . . . Individuals and teams are in control of the variables that they perceive to be important to their success. It's not about the variables that the leader thinks are important, but the variables that the individual or team deems important. Empowerment is in the eyes of the empowered.

✓  *When* . . . Decisions move to their point of implementation. The empowered is the individual or team responsible to do IT. So, the empowered will make the decisions about how and when it will be done. Of course, responsibility is attached to virtually any empowerment contract. Empowered people are expected to produce . . . and history shows that they do!

✓  *When* . . . Individuals and teams "lay out their own work." When the empowered are charged with a responsibility or a project, <u>they</u> determine who will be on the team, how they will organize, the roles of team members, etc. This is not to say that the empowered don't listen. They seek advice and support and are very aware of how their work impacts other parts of the learning community. The empowered are team players dedicated to the learning community's vision.

✓  *When* . . . People express themselves through their work. "By our work they shall know us." Empowered professionals are proud of the contributions they are able to make to their learning community and to their profession.

---

Empowerment is about acknowledging and releasing
the power people and teams already have.

---

Here's our take, and the QL's take, when asked to solve a problem:

### *Empowerment = Go figure it out!*

We leave this section on empowerment with the following figure that says it all.

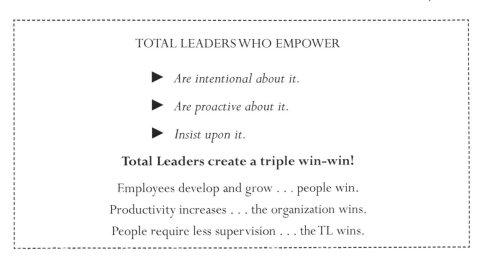

TOTAL LEADERS WHO EMPOWER

▶ *Are intentional about it.*

▶ *Are proactive about it.*

▶ *Insist upon it.*

**Total Leaders create a triple win-win!**

Employees develop and grow . . . people win.

Productivity increases . . . the organization wins.

People require less supervision . . . the TL wins.

**Figure 6.4**

# PR 11: Creating and Using Feedback Loops to Assess MCL Systems and Processes

General Mills boasts of its cereal by boldly stating on the box, "Wheaties, the Breakfast of Champions." Ken Blanchard, leadership guru, doesn't get into a food fight with General Mills, but uses equally strong language when he tells us that, "Feedback is the Breakfast of Champions." For this performance role about "feedback loops," let's assume that Blanchard is right.

In short, feedback is the process that helps us determine the impact of our actions. It provides us with the information we need to determine if and how we should change the way we are doing things in order to improve both our processes and our results. Try as we might, it's hard to think of a situation where we can systematically and continuously improve our performance without having some type of feedback to guide us.

Quality Leaders are intentional about feedback, both when giving it, and when asking for it. They know what they want to measure and improve; they design feedback loops that will provide them with the data they seek; they gather and analyze it; and they make decisions and changes based on their analyses. They also expect everyone in the organization to create feedback loops and establish continuous improvement expectations for themselves as well. That's how recipes get tweaked based on taste, golf swings get altered based on that last errant shot, and dating lines get refined based on refusals or near misses. Those unaware of feedback loops continue making cookies that are not sweet enough, hitting shots that go too far right, and spend many evenings alone.

> You can measure quality but you can't manage quality.
> Quality is an output. You can only manage systems.
>
> **W. Edwards Deming**

*Saint W. Edwards Deming* isn't really a saint. We, and all of Japan, just refer to him as such. General MacArthur sent Deming to Japan after WWII and charged him with helping Japan to rebuild its manufacturing infrastructure. Japan, known at the time for crappy (yes, that's the right word) products, was soon sending us Hondas that never seemed to break down or wear out. Deming left us a number of years ago at the age of 94, still doing four-day, 6-hour per day training sessions. He was easily the guru's guru of the quality movement. He made "Feedback Loops," "TQM" (the Total Quality Movement), and "Continuous Improvement" part of every leader's vocabulary. We tell you that about Deming because we are going to use his quote above to frame the remainder of the Feedback Loop PR. Let's take a look at that quote again.

*A golfing story, non-fiction: (cjs) I have a 15 handicap and of course want to get better at the game. I average about 85 strokes for 18 holes. Did I just give you a measure of my "quality?" Well yes. I usually shoot about 85 . . . not as good as 81, but better than 89. (Tiger or Annika are not shaking in their golf shoes.) Will knowing that I average 85 help me to "manage my game?" That is, will knowing about the 85 score help me to improve my game, to get a lower score? No. Like Deming says, "you can measure quality, but you can't manage quality. Quality is an output." Quality is the result of your processes, your people, and your resources.*

Think ahead . . . your school has a 30% dropout rate. That's a measure. But does that measure tell you what you need to change to lower that dropout rate? No, don't think so!

*Back to golf: I took three lessons at Golftec (another great example of mass customizing), a company that wires you up so that it can compare your stance and swing with that of a successful professional golfer with body characteristics close to yours. They put me on the big split screen next to the pro, and in slo-mo, allowed me to make some comparisons. Not flattering! My next two lessons were about changing my swing. At four points in each of my swings, I was presented with data regarding how I compared with the pro. Feedback loop? Yes. Good one? Yes. Objective, usable, behavior changing feedback. My swing is not my score. It is a "system" I use to get a score. Improve the system, and I trust that I will improve my score. My swing can be managed.*

**Back to the dropout problem:** What are the "systems" that we manage that have the potential to lower the dropout rate? What if we were to compare the "would-be dropout" with the learner who is trucking along, doing just fine, and not a dropout candidate? The learner who is doing just fine is being met at his learning level . . . let's say, about 60% of the time. The dropout candidate may be at a 10% level. Much of what he is asked to do is well over his head. Let's jump right in here with MCL that *meets every learner at his/her learning rate every hour of every day*. Might that move the dropout percentage needle? We think so. Let's try that! Let's create a feedback loop for each of our potential dropouts so that we can determine to what degree dropouts are caused by instruction that does not fit the learner's needs. Add learning style, content of interest, and relevant learner outcomes, and we might move that needle much further to the right. These are all instructional practice and processes that we do, that we can manage, that we can change to improve our "quality."

Give the Deming quote another read. Understanding what Saint Deming is saying is key to creating feedback loops that will help the learning community to continuously improve its quality.

**Back to golf:** *After the three lessons at Golftec I had an improved golf swing. The feedback I received, the practice with continuing feedback, and the supportive coaching I received seemed to be working. But I was hitting the ball into a net about 10 yards from the tee. I needed real world feedback. How far was I hitting the ball with my new swing, how straight was I hitting the ball, what might my "quality"/score for 18 holes be? To answer those questions I had to go to the driving range and the golf course. My feedback loops were immediate in the real world. Goodness, there were water, trees, and sand traps there. But I am about 15 yards longer off of the tee . . . and I don't hear that many "tee hees" from my golfing friends. In a year or so, I expect to drop that handicap to 13 or so.*

## FEEDBACK LOOPS FOR THE IMPLEMENTATION OF THE MCL VISION

Certainly, creating feedback loops for a MCL learning community is significantly more complex than the two examples we shared. But the analytical thought process is quite the same.

**An insight** (that should have been obvious): For two years and two books, we have been harping at the Industrial Age assembly line and how that time-based structure is not consistent with what we know about learners and learning. Beginning with a large blank "clean sheet" that didn't already contain Industrial Age assumptions or structures, we were able to make the needs of the learner our starting point. What an OTB opportunity!

We want to be clear that we know that the MCL Vision proposed in *Inevitable* is not perfect, that it will need to be modified as we apply it to real learners, real professional educators, and real settings. When we began the vision building process, no holds barred, we were obligated to be:

> true to learners first,
> true to professional educators second, and
> true to "administrative convenience" a distant third.

The MCL Vision is true to that prioritization. Great success will follow when we do what the MCL Vision suggests.

With that insight in mind, the first feedback loop to design is about the degree to which you are implementing the vision. (We will be more specific in the following Creating Feedback Loops section.) As you become more complete and competent with the "processes" of the MCL Vision, your "quality" will increase. You will have more motivated learners able to demonstrate complex life role outcomes, and achievement data will increase. You will have fewer dropouts, more pleased parents, proud professional educators, and an appreciative community.

In short, your first feedback loop will not be about "doing the right thing." You will assume that you are. You will be concerned with "are we doing the thing," the MCL Vision thing. We fear that as the Inevitable Vision gains traction, somewhere down the line, people will say, "Oh, that Mass Customized Learning thing, we tried that back in the teens and it didn't work," when you had not actually tried it at all. That you had thought about what needed to be done, did it piecemeal, and exited when things got difficult.

## CREATING FEEDBACK LOOPS: SIX STEPS

Creating a feedback loop is a very logical but somewhat complex process. Whether producing widgets or educating children, there are six steps to designing and implementing a sound feedback process. School systems that have clearly defined their learner outcomes and performance standards, and who have built a system for authentically assessing them, will have a head start in creating feedback loops that are objective, meaningful, and growth producing. The six steps are:

1. ***Clearly identify the product/service.*** This is the "quality" dimension of Deming's earlier quote. If, in the end, we want to move the quality needle to

the right, we have to be clear about what our "product" is and what a "quality" product is. While some educators might struggle to identify their product, the verdict is already in: it's *student learning.* It has little to do with seat time. When educators have clearly defined learner outcomes, our product is student *demonstrations of those outcomes* – their learning!

2. *Set quality standards with a heavy-duty focus on customers and clients.* For educators, quality standards often come in the form of rubrics that help educators determine the degree to which learners' demonstrations of learning meet predetermined high-level performance criteria.

3. *Identify the data needed to measure quality standards.* For learning facilitators, this data may be the number or percentage of learners who are demonstrating particular outcomes at a given level of proficiency.

Given the position we took in "An Insight" earlier, we are going to make some "MCL Vision implementation" feedback loop suggestions that fit with Step 3. Let's assume that you have completed your Strategic Design and have momentum going for the implementation of the MCL Vision. Your concern, and the concern of your board and leadership team is, "to what degree are we implementing our vision?" So, what might you want to know? What data do you want to gather? A place to start would be to look at your vision statements. What do you want to occur for learners, for curriculum, for instruction, for assessment, etc. The short list that follows is not exhaustive. You will quite likely be concerned about other implementation factors as well. But for now, let's assume that you want:

- Your curriculum written in a learner outcome format. Data needed: The number and percentage of learner outcomes that are written for each arena of living. (This assumes that you will have life role learner outcomes.)
- Learning facilitators to experiment with customized learning opportunities for learners. Data needed: number and percentage of learning facilitators experimenting with MCL for each learning center.
- Learning center leaders showing strong support for the learning center vision. Data needed: number and names of those showing strong support and those not showing strong support.
- Elementary schools moving toward teaming, non-grading, and multi-age grouping. Data needed: number of teams operating in each learning center.

Leaders of course would already know why they want that data, what they expect that data to show, and how that data will be used.

4.  ***Determine how to collect, analyze, and communicate the data to all decision makers.*** This step requires decisions about where and how learners will be assessed, how the performance data will be compiled, what form the report will take, who is to receive the data, and when to expect that the data will be available for review, study, and analysis.

The "how" questions regarding collection, analysis, and communication are quite straightforward and should not require further explanation. However, Quality Leaders are always alert as to who should have access to what data and under what circumstances. A caution here: Data in the wrong hands, misunderstood or misused, might be harmful. Data should only go to those with "a need to know."

5.  ***Establish a process to ensure that the data is being used effectively.*** Just because people are receiving student performance data doesn't mean they are using it, or using it effectively. If the feedback received isn't used for making focused improvement decisions, then the previous steps have been a waste of time.

A Little Story *(bmcg) I am reminded of a "defining moment" in my professional life. I think we all should be able to identify those moments, learnings, mentors that changed who we are as professionals. One such moment for me was a couple of decades (or more!) ago sitting in the audience when I first heard Larry Lezotte of The Effective Schools Research fame. He was presenting The Seven Correlates of Effective Schools one of which is "Frequent Monitoring of Student Progress."*

*A teacher asked him what he meant by "frequent." "How often," she asked, "should we monitor student progress? Every week? Once a month? Every day?" Good question, I thought. His answer stays with me today . . . It changed me. He said, "Monitor as often as you think you can adjust instruction. Because if you are not planning to adjust instruction, don't bother monitoring." Oh. How kids are doing is feedback to me, the teacher. Oh!*

*Point of this story: Performance data is feedback to US, the educators, telling us if our structures, policies, and practices are working: that students are being successful.*

Data gathering is time consuming and only worth that time if it is being used to improve the processes being applied by the learning community.

A Little Story *(cjs) Our principals were complaining loudly about all of the forms they had to complete for the State Department of Education. I asked them to list what they were being asked/told to submit, and it did seem like a heavy load. The next time I had to go to the State Department I took their list and went to the offices to which the reports were sent. I talked with the secretaries in each office about how those reports were used, and more pointedly, IF they were used. More than 50% were never used. Now we didn't want to get into trouble with the State Department so we continued to submit the reports as requested. But the reports not used were done by a secretary, with a concern for speed and little concern for accuracy. Principals continued to submit those reports that were actually used and were careful of the quality of the data they submitted. I shared my experience and strategy with the State Superintendent. Not much changed. Point of this story: use it, use it wisely, or stop doing it.*

6. **Continuously improve the effectiveness of the process of production and the effectiveness of the feedback loop.** This step is why one does the previous five steps, and it's the focus of Performance Role 12.

Quality Leaders know that feedback loops are the backbone of continuous improvement. What Deming and his colleagues taught the Japanese about quality and feedback after World War II is more necessary in schools today than it is at Toyota or Nordstrom.

Now let's take this six-step process to a school district and look at hypothetical data that could well have emerged from implementing Steps 1-5 above. Let's assume that the data indicates that some students aced the test, some did very well, the largest group was in the average category, some were below average, and some just didn't get it. It would be easy to just give them all "appropriate" grades and encourage them to try harder next time. But this district happens to be led by a Quality Leader who embraces feedback, change, and continuous improvement. She brings her professional teachers together to analyze the student performance data and finds that everyone sort of expected this. No big surprises. Her question to them is critical:

*"Why wasn't every student able to demonstrate the intended level of learning at the conclusion of this learning opportunity?"*

If the learning facilitators in this group are truly professional, and we expect that they are, they will offer answers that open the door to Step 6, and the performance improvement process can unfold from there. Mass Customized Learning is of course the obvious answer.

# PR 12: Continually Improving the Learning Community's Performance

The MCL Vision is THE quality approach to learning, to education. From the very beginning, the vision was created and designed with quality in mind. Learners (read, all learners) are met at their learning level and are motivated to achieve at their most efficient and effective pace. The structure, the policies, the processes, and the practices of MCL are all aligned with learner learning in mind. The vision makes professional leadership possible and an expectation. It allows learning facilitators to be the professionals they desire to be. Everything regarding quality is set. The Quality Leader should be pleased and proud.

But, all of that is vision. When the learners and the learning facilitators show up and begin to put that vision into practice, there will be a need for "Continually Improving the Learning Community's Performance." The Quality Leader expects problems, glitches, and some failures. That IS how we learn, that IS how we get better. We just learned another way not to do it! A learning curve is to be expected.

Logic has it that if we continue doing things the way we always have, we'll probably get about the same results we've always gotten. So, improving organizational performance is directly dependent on modifying what Deming labels, "the process of production." MCL goes beyond "modifying" Industrial Age structures, policies and practices. It transforms them, transforms them to get quality results for every learner, every learning center, and every learning community.

## BASIC, BUT COMPLEX PROCESSES TO SUPPORT MCL

Many of the "processes of production" that the MCL Vision requires of us are new and complex. We believe that technology will help us with all of these processes. These "new ways of doing things" require in-depth planning, close monitoring as they are put into practice, and a readiness to modify them when there is a glitch. We will learn much from the experiences of our innovators who are gearing up to make MCL a reality in their learning community. Some processes that are easily understood but complex in their reality include the processes for:

- Determining how a learner outcome is best learned
- Getting all learner outcomes best learned online, online
- Creating and scheduling seminars for those outcomes requiring interaction
- Designing and implementing the technology that allows learners, learning coaches, and parents to create and monitor the learning plan

- Designing the technology to track the physical location of each learner
- Designing and creating an ePortfolio for each learner

This list will get longer. And one can be assured that nothing this complex will be implemented without problems. The Quality Leader stops, works with his people to locate the part of the process that caused the problem, they fix the problem, flip the switch and the process begins operating again. Over time, these processes will become the new routine, they will smooth out, and the quality of learning opportunities will increase. Only to be changed again when we learn of better ways to do things. Tis the nature of the day for the QL.

Quality Leaders acknowledge, accept, and embrace that quality cannot be improved without improving the process – and "trying harder" doesn't qualify. The structure and the processes embedded in the MCL Vision hold great promise for improving quality, improving results, improving learning, improving the learning experience. We must give it our best shot.

## "GETTING THE RIGHT PEOPLE ON THE BUS, AND THE WRONG PEOPLE OFF THE BUS"

The often heard quote that labels this section is from the bestseller book titled *Good to Great* by Jim Collins. Acting on this short, clear message is critical for the QL. Education is a "people business" and the QL understands that. She is focused on learners first, but knows that the quality of those who work with and for learners is critical to everyone's success. With all of that in mind, the QL is aware of the impact that selection (*the right people on the bus*) and outcounseling (*the wrong people off the bus*) is to the ultimate success of the learner.

---

**STAFF SELECTION**

is the most important decision you will make . . .

It is the quickest way to build capacity . . .

Spend the time to hire the best
or spend 100 times that amount cleaning up the mess!

---

## SELECTION

The QL realizes that hiring personnel begins long before a candidate is sitting in her office waiting to be told if he will be her, and the learning community's, choice. Why is Bob, this candidate, the QL's final choice? How did it all begin? The selection process started with *attracting* the right candidate. When Bob saw the opening, he knew he wanted to be part of this learning community with a reputation for quality, innovation, a learner-centered culture, opportunity, and professional development. (Truth be known, that good salary schedule and access to skiing may also have played a part in Bob's decision to apply.) If the best people don't apply, you don't get the opportunity to select them. The QL knows that the reputation and image of her learning community is her draw, she talks up her learning community at every opportunity. Good people want to be part of their success story.

> A Little Story *(cjs)* When leaving the superintendency after eight years of what I thought to be a very successful and rewarding experience, I decided to do an "exit interview" with each of the twelve members of the leadership team, most of whom were school principals. I asked each of them to share with me what they thought was the one thing that we, as a leadership team, had done that had the greatest impact on our success. There were many things from which to choose; we HAD been successful. My leadership didn't get one vote, our teacher selection process got them all.
>
> We had taken Covey's advice, "If it's important, it should be intentional." We had worked with Selection Research Incorporated (now known as Gallup) to implement the Teacher Perceiver as our interview process. The training to apply the interview process, backed by convincing research, was lengthy and vigorous. We created a feedback loop to determine if the process was working, and over a period of five years significantly upgraded our staff.

In short, getting good people on the bus is the most impactful decision made by the Quality Leader.

---

### Ask Yourself:

▶ *Will this person be excited . . . most mornings anyway . . . to come to work?*

▶ *Will this person be excited about the kind of work he / she will be doing here?*

▶ *Do the values and vision of this person match those of our learning community?*

**The Total Leader will want three loud YESES!**

---

The _selection process_ is exciting and impactful, but Collins also challenges us (and the QL insists) that we "get the wrong people off the bus." Those three "Ask Yourself" questions apply to those already in positions in our learning community. The numbers and the ratio of poor performers are not large, but we must face the fact that some people are just not cut out to be learning facilitators or learning center leaders. Add to that, the critical role that learning facilitators play in the success of learners, and the tough decisions to outcounsel poor performers cannot be dodged.

## OUTCOUNSELING

What should we do with someone who does not perform, or even someone who is very average and doesn't show a growth curve? Educators tend to be kind, forgiving, and tolerant . . . which can get a leader into trouble at times. Our position, and the position we took when we supervised other educators, is that education is the most important profession. Learners deserve highly capable learning facilitators and learning coaches. It is unfair to learners, and professionally unethical for leaders, to retain a person who is not performing. The underperformer must be released/_outcounseled_, always with dignity, of course. The difficult task of removing the poor performer must be addressed.

Although outcounseling a colleague is difficult, long term it is a win-win-win. The outcounseled win when they have the opportunity to move to a role more fitting to their values and talents. The QL doesn't expect to be thanked for this opportunity, but our experience indicates that helping people find a role right for them is healthy for all. Short-term pain for long term job satisfaction. The profession wins when the public realizes that tenure does not trump talent. And of course, the biggest winner of all is the learner who deserves learning facilitators and coaches who are talented, skilled, and professional.

The Quality Leader must be an advocate for the learner. As much as we love educators, QL's must understand that we are not in the "employment business," we are in the "learning business." This obligation is not only for learning facilitators, but for leaders as well. Everything suggested in these statements is applicable to those in leadership positions and throughout the total organization.

Our basic beliefs regarding outcounseling:

- Education is the most important profession.
- Educators are moral people who believe strongly in the mission of education.
- Our greatest challenge is to keep the great educators in the profession.
- Those needing to be outcounseled are a small minority.

*Good to Great* by Jim Collins is a good read for the Total Leader, and the quote with which we began this section included another bit of advice for the QL. Collins said that we should "get the right people on the bus, the wrong people off the bus, **and** the right people in the right seats." So Collins was talking with us about <u>selection</u>, <u>outcounseling</u>, **and** <u>promotion</u>. Beware of promoting people from a role in which they are succeeding to a role that is not a fit. We are most comfortable and most successful when we are in the chair that fits, fits our passion and our talents . . . and that chair should not be a "La-Z-Boy."

We leave you with more insights from Jim Collins about those people decisions:

1.  When in doubt, don't hire . . . keep looking.
2.  When you know you need to make a "people" change, act.
3.  Put your best people on your biggest opportunity, not your biggest problem.

**Good To Great, Jim Collins**

# REFLECTION: ASSESS AND PLAN

The following self-assessment rubrics (Figures 6.5 – 6.8) might help you to reflect on your knowledge and skills related to *The Quality MCL Leader* and to focus your professional development.

**Reflection Question 1 (Quality Leadership)**

| I. SELF ASSESS<br>(How am I doing?) | What is the degree to which I understand<br>Quality Leadership? |
|---|---|
| 4 INNOVATING | *I can help others understand the role of Quality Leadership, its function within the Total Leaders Framework, how it is necessary for productive change.* |
| 3 APPLYING | *I seek feedback on and reflect on how I am doing as a Quality Leader.* |
| 2 DEVELOPING | *I can explain the values, Principles of Professionalism, and Performance Roles of Quality Leadership.* |
| 1 BEGINNING | *I can identify the characteristics, the mindset, and examples of Quality Leadership.* |

| II. PLAN FOR IMPROVEMENT<br>(What do I need to do?) | III. SUPPORT RESOURCES<br>(Where can I get help?) |
|---|---|
| *What are strategies that I will do to improve my understanding of Quality Leadership?* | *What and/or who are resources that will help me to improve my understanding of Quality Leadership?* |

**Figure 6.5**

**Reflection Question 2 (Quality Leadership)**

| I. SELF ASSESS<br>(How am I doing?) | What is the degree to which I develop and empower everyone to implement the MCL Vision? |
|---|---|
| 4 INNOVATING | *I can help others understand the "triple-win" of empowerment.* |
| 3 APPLYING | *I have created a culture and expectation of teacher as "Learning Facilitator" and "Learning Coach."* |
| 2 DEVELOPING | *I have changed the organizational mindset of professional development from "fixing" to "supporting" everyone as they implement our MCL Vision.* |
| 1 BEGINNING | *I can identify the characteristics of quality professional development.* |

| II. PLAN FOR IMPROVEMENT<br>(What do I need to do?) | III. SUPPORT RESOURCES<br>(Where can I get help?) |
|---|---|
| *What are strategies that I will do to develop and empower everyone to implement the MCL Vision?* | *What and/or who are resources that will help me to develop and empower everyone to implement the MCL Vision?* |

**Figure 6.6**

**Reflection Question 3 (Quality Leadership)**

| I. SELF ASSESS<br>(How am I doing?) | What is the degree to which I create and use feedback loops to assess MCL systems and processes? |
|---|---|
| 4  INNOVATING | *I help others to understand that quality is "the ticket to the game."* |
| 3  APPLYING | *I create feedback loops to determine the degree to which we are implementing our MCL Vision.* |
| 2  DEVELOPING | *I create feedback loops that are objective, meaningful, and growth-producing using the six steps.* |
| 1  BEGINNING | *I understand that "quality" is measured, not managed.* |

| II. PLAN FOR IMPROVEMENT<br>(What do I need to do?) | III. SUPPORT RESOURCES<br>(Where can I get help?) |
|---|---|
| *What are strategies that I will use to use feedback loops to assess MCL systems and processes?* | *What and/or who are resources that will help me to use feedback loops to assess MCL systems and processes?* |

**Figure 6.7**

### Reflection Question 4 (Quality Leadership)

| I. SELF ASSESS<br>(How am I doing?) | What is the degree to which I continually improve the Learning Community's performance? |
|---|---|
| 4  INNOVATING | *I help others to understand that the MCL Vision is THE quality approach to education: improving quality, improving results, improving learning, improving the learning experience.* |
| 3  APPLYING | *I work to "transform" structures, policies, and practices to achieve the MCL Vision, not merely "modifying" current Industrial Age structures, policies and practices.* |
| 2  DEVELOPING | *I expect that a change as complex as MCL will encounter problems and glitches. Undeterred, I work with people to locate and fix problems.* |
| 1  BEGINNING | *I accept and embrace that quality cannot be improved without improving the processes, and "trying harder" doesn't qualify.* |

| II. PLAN FOR IMPROVEMENT<br>(What do I need to do?) | III. SUPPORT RESOURCES<br>(Where can I get help?) |
|---|---|
| *What are strategies that I will do to continually improve the Learning Community's performance?* | *What and/or who are resources that will help me to continually improve the Learning Community's performance?* |

**Figure 6.8**

Chapter 7

# The Service Leader

*Hanging Tough!*

|  | Profile of<br><br>**THE<br>SERVICE EDUCATIONAL LEADER**<br><br>*Leading Compassionately and with Dedication* |
|---|---|
| MINDSET | People are our most valuable asset and they will do the "right thing right" if they get our consistent support. When we make our MCL Vision a reality, it will be because of our people. |
| PURPOSE | To support the change to MCL by aligning the learning community's expectations, policies, structures, and reward systems with our MCL Vision. |
| CHANGE BELIEF | The MCL Vision will come to be, and be sustained, when people are supported and rewarded for making vision-directed change. |
| PERFORMANCE ROLES | ▶ Rewards positive contributions to the MCL Vision<br>▶ Restructures the instructional delivery system to meet learner needs<br>▶ Manages the learning community's MCL Vision |
| PERSONAL VALUES | Risk Taking<br>Teamwork |
| PRINCIPLES | Alignment<br>Contribution |
| THE GURUS | Ken Blanchard and Robert Greeleaf |
| THE EXEMPLARS | Mother Teresa and Paul Newman |
| KEY SOURCES: | • *Leading at a Higher Level,* Ken Blanchard, 2006<br>• *Execution: The Discipline of Getting Things Done,* Larry Bossidy and Ram Charan, 2002<br>• *Servant Leadership,* Robert Greenleaf, 1991<br>• *The Power of Alignment,* George Labovitz and Victor Rosansky, 1997<br>• *The Servant,* James Hunter, 1998 |

# THE SERVICE LEADER

## Supports the Implementation of the MCL Vision

*"The main thing, is to keep*
*The main thing the main thing!"*

### George Labovitz and Victor Rosansky

*Being Keeper of the Dream, Keeper of the Vision*
*is at the core of Service Leadership.*

There are so many right-on, hard-hitting quotes available to begin talking about the Service Leader . . . we had trouble limiting ourselves to two. The first is a match to the earlier quote, "The Main Thing is to Make the Main Thing the Main Thing." That statement, that directive, was about the Strategic Direction side of the TL Framework. The advice for the Strategic Alignment side of the framework has the same ring, "The Main Thing is to *Keep* the Main Thing the Main Thing."

Public schools, and organizations in general, have a much better track record with the advice regarding *Making* the Main Thing than *Keeping* the Main Thing. Many thick, heavy, dusty Strategic Plans in three-ring binders remain on the bookracks in the superintendents' offices. That seems to be the norm; that's the problem. Creating the Strategic Plan was . . . well, creative. Everyone left the planning session with great feelings for their planning accomplishments and about the promise this plan had for improving their system.

But upon returning to the office on Monday morning, reality sets in. There is a long list of emails demanding attention, a calendar for the week that is packed due to those three days at the Strategic Design Workshop, and a personnel problem that needs immediate attention. That is the real world. We have been there. However, no matter what, *alignment must take precedence and begin* before the emails. Stephen Covey's Habit #1, "Putting First Things First," defines it as "what's important and what's urgent." It is time to "cowboy up" and . . . now *keep the main thing the main thing!* The leader can choose to either do the important things or the urgent things. Sometimes the urgent things are so urgent that they need to be done, but if the leader only does the urgent, the important will never get done.

Your Strategic Design, professionally designed in a 15 page pamphlet, will fit into your iPad holder. You can carry it everywhere you go. No chance of the "gathering dust" thing because you refer to it whenever making a decision – especially when you are in the presence of others. (Remember the Modeling Performance Role in Authentic Leadership?) Doing that keeps you honest and makes others think and say, "The Sup is SERIOUS about this MCL thing!"

The key word in the second quote is "keeper." You have that charge. If you don't do it, no one else will take the vision seriously. You will need and want help of course. Time to think about the leadership team, as a group and as individuals. Are they outwardly, loudly, constantly talking up the MCL Vision and "publicly" using it as a decision screen? As keeper of the vision, let them know that that is an expectation. (This might also be a great time for the leadership team to work through the Supervision for Alignment module. Go to our website, www.masscustomizedlearning.com, for resources for Inevitable Too!)

## DIALOGUE STARTERS FOR THE SERVICE LEADER

When everyone who reports to you understands and is committed to the MCL Vision, the organizational chart gets stood on its head and the Service Leader is "in service" to everyone who once was in the line of boxes beneath her name and position. The Service Leader is in the business of serving those who are working to make the vision a reality. The following four conversation dialogue starters will help you as you assume your supporting role as Service Leader:

1. *"Hey Linda . . . I appreciate what you do for our learners and for our learning community."*

    It's always good to begin a conversation with a positive statement, but that positive statement must be authentic.

    *"I'm really excited about our MCL Vision and what it will mean to our learners. Tell me, what are you doing in your learning center / learning*

*team/department to help us implement our vision, to make our vision real for learners?"*

React positively to almost anything she says. If her MCL activities are minimal, be ready to make suggestions as to how the vision should be impacting her role/position.

2. *"Tell me about the vision you have for your learning center/team/ department."*

Everyone should/must have a personal and/or team vision that is aligned with the vision of the learning community. Again, compliment and show gratitude for those visions aligned with MCL, but be ready to do some coaching about what the vision might/should be if the response to the question is weak.

3. *"Thank you for what you do for our learners and for what you are doing to help us become a MCL system. Tell me, what can I do, or stop doing, that will support you as we work toward customizing learning for each learner?"*

The Service Leader is open and honest when asking this question. She listens, paraphrases what she heard, responds regarding what she will do or stop doing, jots a note to herself on her Surface Pro, returns to her office, and has the promise that she made in the school mail the next morning. The word gets around: *When you ask the Supt./Learning Center Leader for something, she actually listens, makes a note, and delivers*

4. *"What seems to be working for you? Where are you meeting with your most meaningful successes?"*

Service Leaders are positive and optimistic. Their glass is half full . . . actually a bit over half. Everyone likes to be asked about their successes . . . especially by their Total Leader.

# THE PRAGMATIC SERVICE LEADER

Superintendents and Learning Center Leaders are charged with leadership and management. We have expectations of them. They have authority simply because of their positions. What "buttons" are they able to push to make things happen, to make change happen, to make the MCL Vision a reality? In short, how do they align their position and influence with the MCL Vision?

Let's be systematic about this alignment process. We have grouped the "buttons" into categories that rather closely match the Leadership Domains. How are you doing on each "button?" Which would rate a five, and which need work?

# PURPOSE

- **Mission Statement:**
  *Do you have one? Is it clear, challenging, and inspirational? Is it obviously in alignment with the MCL Vision?*

- **Learner Outcomes:**
  *Do you have explicit learner exit outcomes? Do you know what you want graduates to know, be able to do, and be like when they walk out your doors?*

- **Vision:**
  *Have you created a concrete picture of what your learning community will look like, feel like, and be like when you are operating at your ideal best, when you have fully implemented the MCL Vision?*

# OWNERSHIP

- **Involvement:**
  *Are you including those impacted by your decisions in the decision making process?*

- **Commitment:**
  *Are you identifying and communicating the WIIFYs (What's in it for you.) for each role group impacted by the MCL Vision?*

- **Political Support:**
  *Have you "sold" the MCL Vision to the powerful political groups in your community?*

- **Labor Relations:**
  *Have you acquired the support of the teacher association for the MCL Vision? Are you helping learning facilitators to know and understand the WIIFYs for their profession?*

- **Culture:**
  *Have you been "intentional" and systematic about creating a change-friendly culture? Do you have a systematic process for monitoring the culture of your learning community?*

# CAPACITY

- **Staff Selection:**
  *Have you aligned your staff selection process with the MCL Vision? Do you consciously and systematically select new hires based on the beliefs, values, and skills required to create and maintain a MCL system?*

- **Professional Development:**
  *Are professional development opportunities aligned with the new roles of learning facilitators and learning center leaders? Are there attractive learning opportunities available for learning facilitators and learning center leaders?*

- **Staff Collegiality:**
  *Are learning facilitators encouraged to form collegial teams? Does the system "reward" teaming and collegiality? Is "teaming" thought to be a force for professional development?*

- **Technology:**
  *Is technology being used to transform the structure of learning centers and the learning community? Do curriculum and instruction leaders team closely with the IT leaders? Do learners have access to online learning opportunities?*

# SUPPORT

- **Curriculum Development:**
  *Is the learning community's curriculum being written in learner outcome format? Are learner outcomes designed to be measureable? Do curriculum, instruction, and technology people work as a team to create learning opportunities for learners?*

- **Learner Assessment:**
  *Are learners being advanced when they have demonstrated learner outcomes? Is your system moving toward an electronic portfolio for each learner? Have you changed your grading system from a rewards & punishment system to a feedback & progress system?*

- **Instructional Delivery:**
  *Is every learner every hour of every day met at his learning level? Is the curriculum delivered in a "how is this outcome best learned" manner/method?*

- **Risk Taking:**
  *Does your learning community culture promote innovation and "good shot" risk taking? Are your people trying new ways of doing things? Do you reward your innovators/risk takers?*

- **Policies and Procedures:**
  *Have you consciously and systematically aligned board policies and procedures to be supportive of the MCL Vision? Is the board outwardly supportive of the MCL Vision for your learning community?*

- **Budget:**
  *Do the form, the vocabulary, and the level of expenditures of the learning community budget clearly indicate that it is a budget designed to implement and maintain a MCL system?*

This listing is a good start, however you may want to add "buttons" of your own. Also, you may want to share your assessment with the leadership team and your staff. Of course, not all "buttons" are created equally. You will want to choose the "buttons" that have the most powerful impact, the ones that will give your vision the biggest boost. Leverage points. Covey's teachings continue to ring true here. We think his "Putting First Things First" means you must prioritize.

## EVERYONE! "ON THE BUS!"

We have worked with businesses, educational systems, and other not-for-profits. We know that change is difficult. But nowhere is change more difficult than in public education. We are entrenched. Everyone in our community knows what schools should be like. They went to one. They remember Mrs. Dunbar's fifth grade class where she opened each afternoon with a chapter from a good storybook, how Mr. Hageland taught biology in a way that made us all want to become doctors, and how playing basketball provided a reason to stay in school. Thinking outside-the-box is hard for everyone, even our most innovative tech gurus. Just try to change schools . . . just try!

Businesses know that they must change to compete. They believe CEO Jack Welch when he says, "If you're not changing at least as fast as the world around you, you are about to go out of business." When the leadership's vision for a business changes, people are asking, "What does this mean for me?" And there is a bit of fright in their voices. There is an urgency to get on board – to better the company, the organization, or the product. Historically, many educators looked at a new vision, and said, "Some good ideas here." Or, "Well, that's an option." There was no sense of urgency – even with the threat of charter schools skimming off our clientele. We believe that times have changed . . . and changed for many educators as well. They _see_ the need for change, for significant change, for transformational change. They see the MCL Vision as the change we need NOW.

The Total Leader and his role mate, the Service Leader, make some assumptions about the need for change and for the need to have "everyone on the bus." Basically, the logic goes like this. If the MCL Vision is best for learners, if the mission, values, learner outcomes, and vision were created through a legitimate process that involved all role groups in the community, implementing the vision is not "optional" *to anyone*. We can't make the significant changes that must be made while pulling a load of resisters. The Service Leader expects that everyone will be on the bus. Jim Collins, in his bestseller *Good to Great*, made the case that: "Level 5 leaders get the right people on the bus, the wrong people off of the bus, and the right people in the right seats." This may sound a bit too bold, but we are leading the most important organization in the community; we need everyone aligned with where we want and need to go.

# MORAL FOUNDATION OF THE SERVICE LEADER

The Service Leader is about action, about making things happen, about advancing the MCL Vision. He was a "leader" when he set that compelling Strategic Direction and created that inspirational vision; he had one foot on each side of the direction/alignment continuum when he created a commitment to the vision; and now he is a skilled "manager" as he develops the capacity to change and supports the people who are doing "the heavy lifting" of implementation. The Service Leader knows how to get things done! His values and principles are keys to alignment and productive change.

# VALUES OF THE SERVICE LEADER

- **Risk Taking:** extending beyond the tried, true, and familiar to do different things a different way, often without the assurance of success. Risk taking involves taking initiative, innovating, and speaking out.

The statements, "We must be willing to take risks," and "We should not experiment with our children's education," would seem to be at odds. But they are not when done right. Not when MCL is a vision that has not been fully implemented anywhere at this date, but the solid research on which it is based is undeniable. The assembly-line instructional delivery system is inconsistent with almost everything we know about learning and learners. MCL was designed from the beginning to be directly aligned with our most solid research regarding learners and learning. Which is the risk, to continue the assembly line or to "experiment" with MCL?

- **Teamwork:** working collaboratively and cooperatively toward achieving a common recognized end, with individuals going out of their way to make the performance or results of others easier and better.

One knowledgeable, talented, and insightful person can frequently solve problems. Complex problems, however, require <u>teams</u> of knowledgeable, talented, and insightful people. The Service Leader understands the complexity of the MCL Vision in its implementation. We can argue if it "takes a community to raise a child," but we can't argue with the need to have everyone on the bus and working as a team to implement the MCL Vision.

# PRINCIPLES OF PROFESSIONALISM OF THE SERVICE LEADER

- **Alignment:** the purposeful, direct matching of decisions, resources, and organizational structures with the organization's declared purpose, vision, and core values.

This "principle" is a no-brainer for the Service Leader. One important person or one process not aligned with the vision of the learning community creates friction, wasted energy, and resistance. The Service Leader gets every person, every process, and every resource on the "True North" arrow of the compass. All "buttons" and all available "levers" are pushed and pulled to align with the vision target. The Service Leader insists on alignment for himself, and also helps "teams" to follow his "alignment" principle.

- **Contribution:** freely giving and investing one's attention, talent, and resources to enhance the quality and success of meaningful endeavors.

# PERFORMANCE ROLES OF THE SERVICE LEADER

When we defined the Authentic Leader, we asked you a rather "in your face" question, *"How bad do you want it?"* We could hear the "Yeses" and the "Amens" from here! You made the commitment, and we are sending the bill. We are at the "Payment Due" part of the program.

We also suggested earmarking the page that contained the Total Leaders Framework, all on one page. You may want to flip back and forth as we do a quick review of how we came to today's lesson on how "The Service Leader Supports the Implementation of the MCL Vision." The three top boxes in Figure 1.1 in Chapter 1 are about Leadership 101. Strategic Design is about first, setting a Strategic Direction and second, about aligning "everything" in the learning community with that direction. Getting a bit more specific about the leadership required for MCL to happen, we worked through four Leadership Domains that brought us to this point, to the fifth domain, the Service Leader Domain.

As a review: The Authentic Leader created the reason to change; the Visionary Leader painted a concrete picture of the MCL Vision; the Relational Leader created the commitment for the change; the Quality Leader helped us to create the capacity to change, and we are now ready to discuss how the Service Leader provides the support for the change. All nice and tidy, right? Well, not so fast. We again remind you that leadership is a complex undertaking and all of these domains tend to overlap. So, you will be using all of the domains almost every day as well as many of the Performance Roles. The better you understand the domains and the Performance Roles, the better you will be when required to think on your feet about what might be the right thing to do or say given this particular situation. You are a Total Leader; you are ready for this.

Service leadership is shaped through consistent attention to three critical Performance Roles, each of which helps drive organizational alignment:

▶ *Rewarding positive contributions to the MCL Vision*

▶ *Restructuring to allow for MCL*

▶ *Managing the learning community's MCL Vision*

Here is what the Performance Roles look like in action.

# PR 13: Rewarding Positive Contributions to the MCL Vision

*"Leadership*
*The skill of influencing people to work enthusiastically*
*toward goals identified as being for the common good."*

**James Hunter**

James Hunter, in his popular book *The Servant*, clearly states his position that "leadership is a skill," a skill that can be learned and practiced. His quote is an excellent mindset if the Service Leader is to *reward contributions* to the MCL Vision. And, if your Strategic Direction was created as we suggested when we defined Authentic Leadership, you have created "goals identified as being for the common good." Your community is in agreement that the MCL Vision is for the "common good."

Education is a "people" business. Our greatest assets *really are* our people. For Service Leaders, "our people are our greatest asset" is not a slogan; it's a reality. People oriented organizations thrive when they can attract, hire, and retain creative, talented, and responsible people. Daniel Pink in *A Whole New Mind*, and Richard Florida in *The Flight of the Creative Class* tell us about how necessary it is today to employ people who are creative and talented. They also tell us how difficult it is to keep them. TLs no longer hire people who are simply "qualified;" they seek out and select those who are "uniquely talented." In short, Service Leaders continuously seek more effective ways to attract, hire, and retain good people. We re-remind: the selection process is the longest lever the Quality Leader has available to increase "capacity."

It is quite natural for people to do what they get rewarded for doing, and that reward can be something tangible like dollars, or something intangible like "feeling appreciated." Service Leaders are fully aware of this and use both tangible and intangible rewards to keep their team enthused, motivated, and engaged. But Service Leaders do not simply reward people for their enthusiasm, motivation, and engagement. They reward everyone for contributions that are **aligned with and directly support the organization's inspirational MCL Vision.** In doing so, Service Leaders do their best to align three powerful forces that bolster productive engagement:

○ The personal values of individuals,
○ The core values of the learning community, and
○ The rewards the Service Leader controls.

Aligning these three motivators assures the Service Leader of having team members who are both engaged and productive.

## REWARDING TALENT AND CONTRIBUTIONS

In *First, Break All the Rules*, Marcus Buckingham and Curt Coffman identify what their research has shown to be "the core elements needed to attract, focus, and keep the most talented employees." They're all cost free. Expect some surprises. Their findings follow. We have added a note in italics to Buckingham and Coffman's statements so that the "motivators/rewards" are more easily applied to education and the MCL Vision. We love # 10, but wait until you get there!

1. Do I know what is expected of me at work?
   *Do I know my personal role in making the MCL Vision a reality?*

2. Do I have the materials and equipment I need to do my work right?
   *Do I have access to the technology (for learners and for management) to facilitate our MCL work?*

3. At work, do I have the opportunity to do what I do best every day?
   *Am I working to my strengths?*

4. In the last seven days, have I received recognition or praise for good work?
   *Am I getting "atta girls" for my productivity?*

5. Does my supervisor, or someone at work, seem to care about me as a person?
   *Does the Service Leader know or care about my personal life?*

6. Is there someone at work who encourages my development?
   *Does the Service Leader ask about my career plans, does she encourage me to grow?*

7. At work, do my opinions seem to count?
   *Am I part of the decision making process for those decisions that will impact my work? Am I taken seriously?*

8. Does the mission/purpose of my company make me feel like my work is important?
   *Does the reality that education is the world's most important profession lend "meaning" to what I do from day to day? Does the MCL Vision make my contributions even more meaningful?*

9. Are my co-workers committed to doing quality work?
   *Does my team talk about quality . . . quality learning and quality learning opportunities? Do we frequently talk about improving our processes and practices?*

10. Do I have a best friend at work?
    *Do I have a friend who makes my work more meaningful and enjoyable? Do I have many more than one?*

11. In the last six months, have I talked with someone about my progress?
    *Does the Service Leader know of my accomplishments and my growth? Does she help me to align my skills with the MCL Vision? Is there a formal review process?*

12. At work, have I had opportunities to learn and grow?
    *Am I more knowledgeable and more skilled at MCL than I was six months ago?*

These simply stated questions summarize much of what the literature tells us are the "soft" and powerful motivators that foster meaningful work, engagement, and production. And, we repeat, they don't cost money!! However, we must be quick to add that all of these soft motivators lose their power when salaries, benefits, and perks are not competitive with the market. Therefore, it's better to think, "We must pay to get the best, the creative, the talented. But that by itself isn't enough. Once we get them, these twelve soft rewards are what maximize our dollar investment." Since Service Leaders aren't in a position to entice high performance with discretionary bonuses, they'd benefit enormously from consciously, openly, and skillfully acting on these twelve important elements of engagement – and creating expectations that everyone else in the organization should/will too.

## POSITIVE CONTRIBUTIONS

If Service Leaders are to reward positive contributions, they must first be able to spot one. Specifically, they look for contributions consistent with, and aligned with, the organization's declared values, mission, the MCL Vision, and intended results. You won't be surprised by some of the following contributions, but others are new and highly relevant in today's Age of Empowerment:

- **Hard work:**
  Who's doing the heavy MCL lifting around here? Yes, it's a bit old-fashioned, but hard work is still hard work, and not everyone seeks it out!

- **Risk taking and winning:**
  Risk taking and winning happen when we plan well for the implementation of MCL and everything comes together. This powerful combination usually leads to breakthroughs that pave the way for future MCL success.

- **Risk taking, losing, and learning:**
  Our culture has taught us to fear the concept of losing. But losing is an opportunity to learn. If a Total Leader, or anyone for that matter, has never failed, it's obvious that they haven't taken the risks necessary to significantly improve.

- **Committing fully in team efforts:**
  Attention please! We have new cultural icons. Superman has been replaced by 911 first responders.

- **Challenges to the status quo:**
  It takes courage to take on city hall . . . or the boss. That's why most choose to blend in with the norms of the organization. But telling the Total Leader, "*the emperor,*" that he "has no clothes on" is sometimes what's needed to keep the Service Leader, the team, and/or the learning community on track and improving.

- **Doing it on time, with quality, AND a smile:**
  Most good organizations, including schools, are privileged to employ a number of people who continue to do what is expected, with superior quality, and, in the process, make the learning community a better place for everyone.

- **The natural:**
  Some people just seem to have the MCL Vision running through their veins. They are naturals who just seem to have it, to always be "in their element." The Service Leader needs to reward those "naturals" who sometimes work hard but *always* seem to work smart.

Rewards are only rewards if they are perceived to be rewards by the intended "rewardee." Yes, like Shakespeare's "beauty," rewards are in the eyes and heart of the beholder. So when Service Leaders are unsure of how people like to be rewarded for their contributions, *they ask them*. Invariably, employees begin by talking about money as the ultimate reward. Service Leaders know that everyone likes money. However, they also know that money isn't a very good long-term motivator, especially for some one whose basic needs are already being met. That's why they keep the Buckingham and Coffman list of soft motivators handy. Receiving a raise usually makes employees feel good for a week or two, but then it's back to business as usual. However, when the raise comes directly from an influential supervisor . . . and with a short speech about the value of their contribution and a pat on the back . . . it takes on a far more powerful symbolic and motivational value. Chances are the speech and the pat are of far greater value than the dollars that accompanied them.

With the following powerful motivators and messages, the Service Leader encourages people to work at their creative and productive best to implement the MCL Vision.

| THE MOTIVATIOR | THE MESSAGE |
|---|---|
| Recognition | *We want others to know about your success.* |
| Advancement | *Let us help with your career path.* |
| Freedom | *You set the agenda . . . we'll get the resources.* |
| Responsibility | *This is BIG . . . and we need you to do it.* |
| Atta girls / Atta boys | *Way to go! I saw and appreciate what you did.* |
| Influence | *We want you to help us make our big, important decisions.* |
| Dollars | *The learning community shares the rewards of its success.* |

In summary, Service Leaders recognize that the most powerful motivators are free. They work to pay fair salaries and provide fair benefits, and they lobby the learning community to enhance the welfare of their people. But beyond that, they work through the motivators of opportunity, influence, freedom, responsibility, recognition, and empowerment to bring the MCL Vision into tangible form.

# PR 14: Restructuring to Allow for MCL

If you have retained the bureaucratic, Industrial Age assembly line, *you are not doing Mass Customized Learning.*

If you continue to rely on stick and carrot extrinsic rewards to motivate learners*, you are not doing Mass Customized Learning.*

If you think, "how will we teach this learner outcome" rather than think, "how is this learner outcome best learned," *you are not doing Mass Customized Learning.*

Sorry to begin the Restructuring Performance Role with such bold and clear accusations, but the three statements above are gospel for the MCL advocate. <u>The assembly line is what makes our school systems Industrial Age.</u> Relying on extrinsic rewards rather than applying our most basic research regarding learners and learning is what keeps education from being a profession. Focusing on teaching rather than the learner and learning is what makes our schools bureaucratic.

## PURPOSE OF ORGANIZATIONAL STRUCTURES

Bear with us for a bit as we get to the "foundation" of organizational structures. It may appear that we are putting educators down, but most educators have lived with the Industrial Age assembly-line school structure so long that it has vanished, gone from view. We simply accept that is the structure for schools. Many innovative thinkers of the day continue to take the assembly line as a given. We wonder if they even SEE it. It has been so common and so accepted for so long that it has become transparent. They start "school reform" from that position. So all new ideas begin with the blocker of MCL. The work and the writing of our most respected educators of the day also give in to the assembly line. The MCL Vision is "hiding in plain sight." However, many don't see it.

Our present structure, our policies, and our practices have boxed us into a system where:

Specific Students
*of a*
Specific Age
*must learn*
Specific Things
*on a*
Specific Schedule
*in a*
Specific Classroom
*from a*
Specific Teacher
*using*
Specific Materials and Methods
*so that they can pass*
Specific Tests on Specific Dates
**and only then be called "OK!"**

Service Leaders, by contrast, are highly aware that the structure of any system or organization cannot be created or chosen until the organization is clear about its mission, its purpose. We have all heard the phrase that "form follows function." This is just another way of saying that the "structure of an organization follows knowing and considering the purpose/mission of that organization." In short, and to bring it into focus for this Performance Role, our present Industrial Age assembly-line structure was created about 120 years ago. And it worked, kind of, until about 30 years ago.

The Industrial Age economy required about 25% of our learners to be highly skilled, and that's about what our schools were producing. Seventy-five percent of our adult population found low-skilled jobs for wages that allowed for "the good life." Today, those percentages have more than flipped. Today's economy requires about 85% skilled workers and the other 15% need to find jobs that require only minimal skills.

Service Leaders, by contrast, align the organization's structures, the way it does business, with the learning community's vision. And they do so knowing:

- A structure is a tangible, fundamental pattern of organizational action; you can see it and/or watch it.
- Structures are created to accomplish specific organizational ends.
- Structures can be bureaucratic, controlling, and designed for administrative convenience (like today's schools), or they can be flexible and client-centered (read *learner-centered*).
- Structures that accomplish a given end/outcome usually will not work effectively if that end/outcome changes.
- Structures can take on a life of their own, known as institutional inertia, which makes achieving new ends very difficult. For example, the assembly-line instructional delivery structure described makes customizing learning nearly impossible.

MCL Service Leaders understand the need for structures that align with their learning communities to create a system closer to:

> Anyone
> > *can learn*
> Anything
> > *at*
> Anytime
> > *from*
> Anywhere
> > *from*
> World-class experts
> > *using*
> Transformational technologies and resources
> > *to enhance*
> Their personal interests and life fulfillment.

And so, consider the following two basic truths we have learned over time about this *Restructuring to Allow for MCL* Performance Role:

1. If the structure of the organization doesn't change, don't expect the roles and behaviors of the organization's members to change. Service Leaders must see

176

this connection if they're to successfully support and implement the new MCL Vision.

2.  If a school system doesn't replace the Industrial Age assembly-line delivery of instruction with something that allows for learner-centered customization, the impact of its change effort will be no more than "tinkering." Making the change to a customized instructional delivery system is a paradigm shift requiring risk taking of the first order.

## WEIGHT BEARING WALLS: OLD ONES AND NEW ONES

The short history of the MCL Vision began in Illinois when 70+ superintendents came together to discuss Mass Customized Learning and what was holding us back. We used the metaphor of weight bearing walls (WBWs) to identify the components of our present school structure. For those of you who have never significantly remodeled the interior of a house, we provide the Cliffs Notes of WBWs:

- Physical structures must have walls or other supports to hold the roof up.
- When you remodel a house, it is good to know which interior walls are "weight bearing." Not all interior walls are.
- If you are going to remove a WBW, you must apply another support before that wall can be removed.
- If you don't, the roof will cave in . . . duh!

We began by asking the 70+ Lake County, IL superintendents to identify the WBWs of our present . . . and severely outdated . . . Industrial Age instructional delivery system. The superintendents, who surprised us by not being the least bit defensive, came to a consensus that our school structure was held up, held together, by the following ten WBWs:

1.  Grade Levels
2.  Courses/Curriculum
3.  Class Periods/Bell Schedule
4.  Students Assigned to Classrooms
5.  Textbooks
6.  ABC Grading System/Student Evaluation
7.  Learning Happens in Schools/Use of Space
8.  Nine-Month School Year/Agrarian Calendar

9. Report Cards/Informing Parents
10. Paper and Pencil Orientation

Note that each of the 10 WBWs is supported by AND dependent on nearly all the others. If one or two WBWs are removed, the structure will have difficulty in functioning. The WBWs of our system are interdependent. They are buddies. Buddies in cahoots!

This interdependence makes step-by-step change difficult. **It makes it very difficult to tiptoe into MCL.**

MCL has WBWs also, and they are very different from those of the assembly line. Like the assembly line, the MCL WBWs are interdependent. MCL WBWs are not a one-to-one match with the assembly-line WBWs. If they were, we could simply change one WBW at a time.

So what are the MCL WBWs? In Chapter 9 of *Inevitable,* we describe the elements of MCL that must be in place before the learning community is "Ready for Rollout." These "elements" are the equivalent of the assembly line's WBWs. Being ready for rollout requires that your learning community:

1. Has derived a Strategic Design (see Chapter 1)
2. Has written curriculum as learner outcomes
3. Has categorized learner outcomes by learning format (That is, they have answered the question, "How is this outcome best learned?" for each learner outcome.)
4. Has created and placed online learner outcomes online
5. Has created seminars for those learner outcomes requiring an interactive seminar format
6. Has designed and implemented scheduling technology for individual learners (This is big . . . it is the technology that allows Lori to do her learning plan; see *Inevitable*, Chapter 7.)
7. Has designed and implemented technology that allows each learner to create and maintain an electronic portfolio that documents the demonstration of learner outcomes
8. Has designed and implemented accountability technology for administrators

The two lists of WBWs show sharp contrasts.

*Both systems must be organized, managed, and controlled.*

The assembly line organizes, manages, and controls through location and time. We know which students are in English III at 10 AM, we know who the teacher is, and we know the classroom they are in. When Mom calls and needs to talk with Molly, the school secretary has all the information he needs to go get Molly.

MCL organizes, manages, and controls with technology. Anyone with "a need to know" who has Lori's name, student number, or barcode can access her personal and individual learning schedule to find that: Lori is in the First National Bank board room attending the Writing and Defending a Business Plan seminar from 1PM to 3PM.

*Both school principals and learning center leaders are charged with control and safety.*

Principals/leaders will not risk implementing MCL unless they believe that they will retain control of the location of learners and learning facilitators, nor should they. If we look all around us, we see businesses and not-for-profit organizations that organize, manage, and control with technology. Well-known and successful customizing organizations include, but certainly aren't limited to: Visa, iTunes, Amazon.com, Bing, Google, Yahoo.com, Wal-Mart, Pandora Radio, banks, hospitals, etc., etc.

## HIGH SCHOOL RESTRUCTURING: WHAT IF . . .

Join us as we think like a visionary: *how we might get started toward MCL without upsetting the apple cart.* Let's assume that you are the principal of Madison High School and that your school has about 300 learners grades 9 – 12. The following "what ifs" are cumulative, each builds on all previous "what ifs."

- *What if* you had three Math teachers in your Math Department?

- *What if* you . . . remember now, you are the principal . . . believed that the two guys and one gal in the Math Department might be ready to take a risk to significantly improve learning opportunities for ALL learners?

- *What if* they agreed to give MCL a shot in their department?

- *What if* the three Math teachers agreed to eliminate the sharp beginning and ending dates of courses and decided to take the learner outcomes for Algebra I, Algebra II, Geometry, Trigonometry, and Pre-Calculus and place all outcomes on one continuum of Math concepts and skills – creating Mathematics Modules?

- *What if* all learners in your system had one study hall?

- *What if* the principal could organize the master schedule so that all Math learners had one period for Math and that they had their study hall period either right before or right after their scheduled Math class? (Doing this would allow learners two periods for math rather than one, and a study hall if they chose to do so.)

- *What if* the Math teachers, now called learning facilitators, identified which learner outcomes were best learned online and which were best learned via direct instruction?

- *What if* each learner had an ePortfolio that recorded and documented the learner outcomes she had mastered?

- *What if* each Math learner had three options whenever she entered the Math wing . . . she could work online on those outcomes best learned online, she could join a group for direct instruction, or she could ask for peer tutoring help from someone who had successfully mastered that outcome within the past two weeks or so?

- *What if* there were enough computers to accommodate those who needed to work on online learner outcomes?

- *What if* the Math Department created a culture of high expectations, learner responsibility, and supportive professional learning facilitators?

- *What if* Math learning facilitators, using scheduling technology or some other system, could quickly know each hour of every day, which learners required direct instruction, and could use that data to group learners efficiently for direct instruction?

- *What if* the principal were able to give credit for any course at any time when the learner outcomes for that course (old vocabulary) have been demonstrated by the learner?

- *What if* parents could access the records and progress of their learner at any time . . . along with notes of praise or concern from a learning facilitator whenever necessary or appropriate?

- *What if* learners could actually complete more than expected Math modules in their four high school years?

- *What if* more than 30% of your learners graduated with the equivalent of five or more Math courses on their permanent record?

- *What if* each learner had an ePortfolio to verify that he/she had mastered all the required learning outcomes?

- *What if* the English Department wanted to talk with you about how they might join the Math Department in this MCL innovation?

Our point here is not for you to take this listing of "What ifs" to your Math Department. Rather, it is to encourage you to think about how you might find a place to begin MCL. Scenarios like the one above are happening in many elementary and middle schools. Teachers are teaming, creating non-graded, and multi-age groupings to better meet the customizing needs of their learners. Learners are excited, engaged, and *learning*. Learning facilitators are feeling and acting more professional.

We conclude Performance Role 14, *Restructuring to Allow for MCL*, with the challenge to rid your learning community of the assembly-line, time-based organizational structure that is so severely inconsistent with what we know about learners and learning.

# PR 15: Managing the Learning Community's MCL Vision

> *"You can manage yourself.*
> *But you do not manage other human beings.*
> *You manage things, you lead people."*
>
> ### James Hunter

Before we started the actual writing of *Inevitable Too! The Total Leader Embraces Mass Customized Learning*, we agreed on the need to focus on the Performance Roles of the Total Leader. The Performance Roles are where leadership actually happens. The PRs are what leaders DO when they take action. And this was to be a book about action, actions to make MCL happen. We knew what we wanted to include in each of the Performance Roles . . . except for this final PR: *Managing the Learning Community's MCL Vision*. We thought we might be "enlightened" when we arrived at #15.

Well, we may not be "enlightened" at this point, but our serious reflection about what to include in the final PR has led to an insight: We may have said it all! We may have told and maybe over-told you about everything YOU should do.

*We're not bossy; we just know what you should be doing!* ☺

As we concluded the Leadership Domain chapters, we realized that our/your entire book is about **Managing the Learning Community's MCL Vision.** This PR has been detailed throughout. The label for this 15th PR could have been the title for the book. And so, if you are disappointed with the lack of content for this final Performance Role, feel free to re-read *Inevitable Too!*

> After VISION
> It's all about WILL
>
> Education and educators
> must feel the urgency!

# REFLECTION: ASSESS AND PLAN

The following self-assessment rubrics (Figures 7.1 – 7.3) might help you to reflect on your knowledge and skills related to *The Service MCL Leader* and to focus your professional development.

**Reflection Question 1 (Service Leadership)**

| I. SELF ASSESS<br>(How am I doing?) | What is the degree to which I<br>understand Service Leadership? |
|---|---|
| 4  INNOVATING | I can help others understand the role of Service Leadership, its function within the Total Leaders Framework, how it is necessary for productive change. |
| 3  APPLYING | I seek feedback on and reflect on how I am doing as a Service Leader. |
| 2  DEVELOPING | I can explain the values, Principles of Professionalism, and Performance Roles of Service Leadership. |
| 1  BEGINNING | I can identify the characteristics, the mindset, and examples of Service Leadership. |

| II. PLAN FOR IMPROVEMENT<br>(What do I need to do?) | III. SUPPORT RESOURCES<br>(Where can I get help?) |
|---|---|
| What are strategies that I will do to improve my understanding of Service Leadership? | What and/or who are resources that will help me to improve my understanding of Service Leadership? |

**Figure 7.1**

**Reflection Question 2 (Service Leadership)**

| I. SELF ASSESS<br>(How am I doing?) | What is the degree to which I<br>reward positive contributions to the<br>MCL Vision? |
|---|---|
| 4 INNOVATING | *I can help others understand the powerful motivators that foster meaningful work and engagement.* |
| 3 APPLYING | *I reward positive contributions to the MCL Vision through opportunity, influence, freedom, responsibility, and empowerment.* |
| 2 DEVELOPING | *I know and act on the twelve elements of engagement.* |
| 1 BEGINNING | *I can spot contributions that are consistent with and aligned with the MCL Vision.* |

| II. PLAN FOR IMPROVEMENT<br>(What do I need to do?) | III. SUPPORT RESOURCES<br>(Where can I get help?) |
|---|---|
| *What are strategies that I will use to reward positive contributions to the MCL Vision?* | *What and/or who are resources that will help me to reward positive contributions to the MCL Vision?* |

**Figure 7.2**

**Reflection Question 3 (Service Leadership)**

| I. SELF ASSESS (How am I doing?) | What is the degree to which I restructure the instructional delivery system to meet learner needs? |
|---|---|
| 4  INNOVATING | I help others to understand why the Industrial Age structures must change. |
| 3  APPLYING | I align the structures of the organization to the MCL Vision. |
| 2  DEVELOPING | I understand the difference between Industrial Age structures of schools and the Information Age structures of learning communities. |
| 1  BEGINNING | I know what structures are and what they do. |

| II. PLAN FOR IMPROVEMENT (What do I need to do?) | III. SUPPORT RESOURCES (Where can I get help?) |
|---|---|
| What are strategies that I will use to restructure the instructional delivery system to meet learner needs? | What and/or who are resources that will help me to restructure the instructional delivery system to meet learner needs? |

**Figure 7.3**

# The Incongruent Walrus

# THE INCONGRUENT WALRUS

*Congruency: aligning perception and reality.*

*Congruency is the "correlation" between*
*What the **leader perceives he is doing***
*With what **direct reports perceive the leader is doing.***

**Duff Rearick**

We have had two months of reflection and observation time between finishing a rather complete draft of *Inevitable Too!* and writing this epilogue as we ready ourselves for publication. Things are happening. *Inevitable: Mass Customized Learning* created a buzz that is turning into bold steps toward implementation of the MCL Vision. MCL has proven itself to be very desirable to most everyone, and doable to courageous learner advocates. We have watched school districts make great strides toward MCL, and we have watched another school district receive some pushback from a minority of teachers and parents.

## MANAGING THE VISION: REALITIES

During this reflection and observation time, a couple of realities about the transition from "creating the vision" to "managing the vision" have emerged. First reality: Superintendents need to be courageous lead learners, lead teachers, and instructional leaders. There is power in the superintendent position, and a vision so bold as MCL requires that power when the going gets rocky. The superintendent must be seen as leading the vision charge. Assistant superintendents and principals must also be instructional leaders, but without the strong and total support of the CEO, they are vulnerable to factions that will fight for the comfortable "known." So, superintendent, you (and all of us) are in the learner learning business. If learners and learning and transforming our Industrial Age schools are not your passion, the role of superintendent (CEO) will not be what it needs to be. Period!

*The most influential leaders are those with*
*both personal power and position power,*
*who never use their position power,*
*but everyone knows they would if they had to.*

Second reality: Involving all role groups in creating a learning community vision and a comprehensive Strategic Direction is the base for support of the vision and its implementation. It is quite easy to skip the Strategic Direction step when everyone is excited about making changes that have the potential to transform our outdated education system, but skipping the authentic involvement of everyone is a move that can come back to bite you.

## LEADER FEEDBACK

Leadership guru, Ken Blanchard, succinctly states that, "feedback is the breakfast of champions," a takeoff on the old Wheaties cereal slogan. Well, if this is the case, leaders are having unhealthy breakfasts. Reality: leaders struggle to get accurate feedback. No one wants to tell the emperor that he has no clothes. This reality causes us to recall a leadership/management fable that we first read some thirty+ years ago titled "The Ill-Informed Walrus:"

---

### The Ill-Informed Walrus (author unknown)

*"How's it going down there?" barked the big walrus from his perch on the big rock near the shore. He waited for the good word. Down below, the smaller walruses conferred among themselves. Things weren't going well at all, but no one wanted to break the news to the Old Man. He was the biggest and wisest walrus in the herd, and he knew his business and they didn't want to disappoint him or put him in a foul mood.*

*"What will we tell him?" whispered Basil, the walrus XO. He well remembered how the Old Man had raved at him the last time the herd caught less than its quota of herring, and he had no desire for that experience again. Nevertheless, for several weeks the water level in the nearby bay had been falling constantly, and it had become necessary to travel farther to catch the dwindling supply of herring. Someone should tell the Old Man. But who? And how?*

> *Finally Basil spoke up: "Things are going pretty well, Boss," he said. The thought of the receding water line made his heart grow heavy, but he went on: "As a matter of fact, the beach seems to be getting larger."*
>
> *The Old Man grunted. "Fine, fine," he said. "That will give us a bit more elbow room." He closed his eyes and continued basking in the sun.*
>
> *The next day brought more trouble. A new herd of walruses moved in down the beach, and with the shortage of herring, the invasion could be dangerous. No one wanted to tell the Boss, though only he could take the steps necessary to meet the new competition. Basil approached the Old Man. After some small talk, he said, "Oh, by the way Boss, a new herd seems to have moved into our territory." The Old Man's eyes snapped open, and he filled his great lungs in preparation for a mighty bellow. But Basil added quickly, "Of course, we don't expect any trouble. They don't look like herring-eaters to me. More likely interested in minnows. And as you know, we don't bother with minnows ourselves."*
>
> *The Old Man let out the air with a long sigh. "Good, good," he said. "No point in our getting excited over nothing then, is there?"*
>
> *Things didn't get any better in the weeks that followed. One day, peering down from his rock, the Old Man noticed that part of the herd seemed to be missing. Summoning the XO, he grunted peevishly, "What's going on, Basil? Where is everyone?" Poor Basil didn't have the courage to tell the Old Man that many of the younger walruses were leaving to join the new herd. Clearing his throat nervously he said, "Well, Boss, we've been tightening up things a bit. You know, getting rid of some of the dead wood. After all, a herd is only as good as the walruses in it."*
>
> *"Run a tight ship, I always say," the Old Man grunted. "Glad to hear that all is going so well."*
>
> *Before long, everyone but Basil had left to join the new herd, and Basil realized that the time had come to tell the Old Man the facts. Terrified but determined, he flopped up to the large rock. "Chief," he said, "I have bad news. The rest of the herd has left you." The Old Walrus was so astonished that he couldn't even work up a good bellow. "Left me?" he cried. "All of them? But why? How could this happen?"*
>
> *Basil didn't have the heart to tell him, so he merely shrugged helplessly.*
>
> *"I can't understand it," the old Walrus said. "And just when everything was going so well."*

**MORAL:**
**What the Boss likes to hear isn't always what he needs to know.**

Leaders quite naturally and routinely don't get accurate feedback, feedback necessary to make effective decisions. We don't want this feedback reality to sound entrenched, however. Leaders, over time, and based on leadership behaviors, can create a culture of openness and transparency. When everyone knows that the leader desires accurate feedback, no matter how difficult to give and to accept, confident and secure followers are able to talk candidly about the leader's lack of clothes. How the leader responds to negative feedback cues the giver of feedback about how to deal with subsequent communication opportunities. In short, leaders must "earn" feedback. They earn it by sincerely thanking the giver and they bend over backwards to make sure that no one perceives the leader as being vindictive.

That said, leaders who do not take steps to intentionally and systematically create feedback loops are putting their leadership decisions in jeopardy. Jack Welch, arguably the most effective CEO of our lifetime, in *Jack: Straight From the Gut* speaks of a "culture of candor," and how GE used their annual employee survey to find out "how deep in the organization our initiatives were taking hold."

## THIRD PARTY FEEDBACK

Our Pennsylvania Leadership Development Center (PLDC) colleagues have created a process labeled simply "Congruency" which allows a third party to survey the leader and his direct reports and provide anonymous feedback to leaders. This is not a "marketing ad" for PLDC, but you can learn more about the Congruency Process by going to the PLDC webpage (www.pldc.name). An advantage of the PLDC process, however, is that the instrument and process are based on the Performance Roles of the Total Leader as described and detailed in *Inevitable Too!* .

Briefly, the PLDC process includes:

- An agreement between the leader's organization and PLDC on the process and procedures for checking for congruency.
- Gathering data from the leader, leader's reports, selected staff, and any other role groups thought to be critical to the successful implementation of the MCL Vision.
- Analyzing the data to determine the strength of each Leadership Domain and the degree of congruency between the perceptions of the leader and the perceptions of the implementers of the vision.
- Presenting the congruency feedback data to the leader.
- Mentoring the leader as to changes that would create greater congruency between the leader's intentions and the perceptions of MCL Vision implementers.
- Conducting subsequent surveys to provide information to the leader about improvements.

The following two figures will help you understand the PLDC Congruency process. They show how to interpret a congruency graph and response data. A 5-point Likert scale is applied when surveying the responses to 20 questions designed around the 15 Performance Roles. Figure 8.1 shows how the graph might communicate a high degree of congruency. Figure 8.2 shows a low degree of congruency. Note the five Total Leaders Leadership Domains at the bottom of each graph.

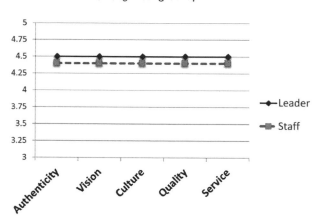

**Figure 8.1**

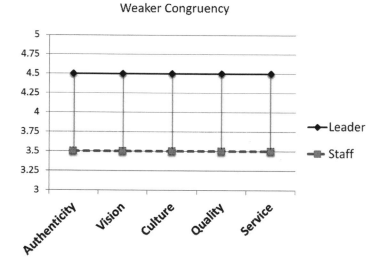

**Figure 8.2**

Figure 8.3 shows an example of what an actual congruency graph might look like. Note that there are varying degrees of congruency between the leader's perceptions of what she is doing and how others perceive her leadership in each of the Leadership Domains. It is quite easy to see how critical it is for leaders to have access to this feedback. The PLDC fable might be titled, "The Highly-Informed Walrus."

## VARIATIONS ACROSS AREAS AND/OR QUESTIONS

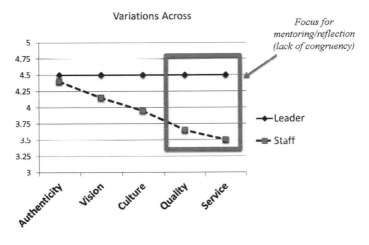

**Figure 8.3**

If you or your organization do not see the need for outside help, or do not have the resources to contract with outside providers, this congruency process can be done in-house. The process is relatively simple to understand, and someone in your system or your community might be contracted to do the work.

Warning: not getting candid and objective feedback about the congruency between leaders' perceptions of reality and followers' perceptions of reality can lead to ill-informed walruses. Total Leaders frequently stop, turn around, and check to see who might be following.

# Thank You

We close our book and our epilogue with a sincere thanks to the many educators who have embraced the Mass Customized Learning Vision. The popularity and potential impact of *Inevitable* has far outdistanced our highest expectations. We see our MCL labels and our ideas for ridding education of the assembly line in the literature everywhere. For us, it frequently feels like we have been passed on the Interstate leading to "meeting the needs of every learner every hour of every day." Our dreams will be realized when the MCL Vision becomes the norm for all learners.

*There are no modest revolutions.*
*There are no modest transformations of school systems either.*

**Jack Welch** paraphrased

# About the Authors

## Charles Schwahn

Chuck is living a rather storybook life . . . by his own admission he has been undeservedly blessed. Chuck has sat in nearly every education chair in his career, has enjoyed them all, and felt success at each step and stop along the way. In retrospect, his career has had three somewhat distinctive roles.

It started with teaching, of course, and moved to leadership at a number of levels. Career segment two was being privileged to consult with and influence educators, business leaders, and not-for-profits throughout the US and Canada. Chuck is living segment three today with the success of *Inevitable: Mass Customized Learning* and his hoped-for success of *Inevitable Too! The Total Leader Embraces Mass Customized Learning.*

Chuck is married to his love, Genny, and lives in the Black Hills of South Dakota in the summer and in the Phoenix area in the winter.

He can be reached at chuckschwahn@yahoo.com.

## Beatrice McGarvey

Bea is a Senior Associate at Marzano Research Lab, a Partner in Total Leaders Associates, and a faculty trainer for International ASCD.

With years of experience as a classroom teacher, middle school counselor, and school and district leader, Bea helps educators around the country to understand *the inevitable*. Her areas of expertise include: teaching for learning, leadership, and organizational development. To her delight, the Mass Customized Learning Vision has moved this work from tinkering with to transforming education.

Bea and her retired-principal-turned-lobsterman husband, Richard, enjoy the beautiful coast of their native Maine while keeping up with her large and growing family. Four grandchildren and nineteen nieces and nephews prove her theory that all children are born with an inherent will and motivation to learn. Her mission, strengthened and validated by MCL, has always been to create learning environments that do not extinguish this natural drive.

She can be reached at mcgarvey@maine.rr.com.